# Designing the Networked Organization

# Designing the Networked Organization

Ken Everett

*With contributions by*
*Richard White*
*Jacqueline Throop-Robinson*
*Roland Spinola*
*Adina Luca*
*and Peter Everett*

Think on Your Feet® is a registered trademark of Think on Your Feet
International, Inc.

First published in 2011 by
Business Expert Press, LLC
222 East 46th Street, New York, NY 10017
www.businessexpertpress.com

ISBN-13: 978-1-60649-195-9 (paperback)

ISBN-13: 978-1-60649-196-6 (e-book)

DOI 10.4128/9781606491966

A publication in the Business Expert Press Strategic Management
collection

Collection ISSN: 2150-9611 (print)
Collection ISSN: 2150-9646 (electronic)

Cover design by Jonathan Pennell
Interior design by Scribe Inc.

First edition: July 2011

10 9 8 7 6 5 4 3 2 1

Printed in the United States of America.

*To Mason A. Carpenter*

# Abstract

Ken Everett proposes the network as the organization of the future, and he wrote this book, with the help of five colleagues, to help the architects of such future organizations.

He started a network of necessity—limited financial resources—but then encountered surprising benefits. He discovered networked organizations to be resilient, innovative, and leader-full and that these characteristics arise out of the *design*. This potential, he says, applies equally to networks of independent associates as it does to traditional organizations willing to adopt a new style of leadership—a style closer to "hosting" than "commanding."

This is a practice-based book: Its developmental model was earned through experience. The model lays out three phases: from connections to communities to coalitions, or from "doing fine" to "getting better" to "getting better at getting better." Ken Everett illustrates these claims with real-life examples. He describes how a family company with only 3 employees grew to be represented in 30 countries via 300 colleagues.

The potential of the networked organization is new, and that's what this book is about.

# Keywords

organization, design, networks, community, resilience, innovation, leadership, engagement, work-life balance, scalability

# Contents

# Preface

The network is the organization of the future, and it may have been the organization of the past: think small-town communities. But global communities are now feasible. We are a family company: 3 employees represented in 30 countries via 300 colleagues. That's what's new, and that's what this book is about.

We started a network because of limited financial resources—it's expensive to open offices in 30 countries. But once started down this track, we encountered benefits we never imagined:

- *Resilience.* This is the ability of the business to weather downturns in the business cycle, whether caused by financial crises, terrorism, tsunamis, or viruses.
- *Innovation.* Nominated by some as the distinctive requirement of the modern organization, we have it in spades, and sometimes uncomfortably so, but we wouldn't change it for the opposite problem.
- *Leadership.* While well-known hierarchies are paying huge sums to recruit superperson leaders, our experience shows networks are full of them.

These pluses are all a function of the *design* of the networked organization, as we will show. And we can add other qualities traditional organizations lust after: high engagement, high quality, low people turnover, better work-life balance, collaboration, low overhead, scalability, natural growth, and more. Not every network shows these. But, and here's a crucial point, the design properties of a networked organization make these all more feasible than models based on hierarchy, command, and control.

However, this is reason to issue a warning: Networked organizations thrive on a different style of leadership. Not all leaders and managers are comfortable with this. I wasn't to start with. This new style is closer to hosting than commanding. And there are more obstacles. The classic military- and church-based organization model is subtly enshrined in our systems, regulations, conventions, language, structures, and education. These combine to create an organizational ecosystem that, at first blush, is more tradition friendly. The business press plays a huge role in this. It devotes significantly fewer column inches to organizations that lack heroes because, as one of its practitioners says, "Noah is a much better story than flood control!"[1]

This book attempts to share the joy, the success, and the sheer humanity of the network alternative. If this interests you, please read on.

# CHAPTER 1

# Introduction

## Designing the Networked Organization

The network can be the organization, and this book suggests a framework for designing such an organization. This chapter lays the groundwork as follows:

- What makes a networked organization?
- What are your answers to three provocations?
- Who is this book for?
- What lies ahead?

## What Makes a Networked Organization?

We suggest three distinguishing characteristics:

1. *Independence.* The members of a network—be they individuals, business units, or companies—enjoy significantly more freedom than their counterparts in traditional organizations.
2. *Community.* A community shares a sense of identity, communication norms, and mutual obligations. The word "community" might sound paradoxical coming after independence, but the paradox is resolved by the next characteristic.
3. *Shared stuff.* This is what unites the independent members. It can be location, interests, protocols, brands, values, passions, or all of these.

This book does not predict the end of the hierarchical, command-and-control organization. It simply invites organizational architects to consider their options before defaulting to traditional choices. The selection made can confer significant advantages. However, if a networked option is selected, and if sustaining the three characteristics listed previously is key to its effectiveness (as we suggest), then leaders need to assume new obligations and roles. These themes—the nature of networked organizations, how to build them, their benefits, and the new roles of leaders—form the core of this book. To kick-start our discussion, I offer three provocations:

1. Arguably, the world's most significant infrastructure achievement is a network. What is it?
2. Up until 2008, the world's largest initial public offering (IPO) was of a networked organization. What was the organization?
3. What is TOYFNET? (This is a trick question.)

## About the Internet

My candidate for the world's most significant infrastructure project is the Internet. You might suggest another—perhaps the pyramids, the air traffic control system, or the Great Wall of China. All have been put forward in the past. But most will agree the Internet is an acceptable candidate. It permeates our lives, professional and private. It is global, innovative, and resilient. Professor Gary Hamel of the London Business School calls it the most successful collaboration in the history of mankind.[1] Whether Hamel's ranking (or mine) is right is beside the point; the Internet is a remarkable achievement.

So what is the secret? The Internet is a global system of networks *all using the same protocols* (the Internet Protocol Suite). It is a *network of networks*. In the 1960s when computer networks first emerged, each had its own protocol and often a special terminal to match. To talk to people on more than one network, you had to leave one terminal, locate another, and log on again. To simplify this clumsy arrangement, protocols for communicating *between* networks were developed. The name "Internet" arose from the idea of internetworking. This collaborative initiative made the whole venture possible.

So who leads the Internet? Few reflect on the fact that the Internet has no CEO and no headquarters. Each constituent network sets its own standards. The shared protocols are maintained by the Internet Engineering Task Force, a nonprofit organization that anyone may associate with by contributing technical expertise. Does this qualify as leadership? It certainly seems so. But if so, it challenges orthodoxy on leadership. Did we, as someone once wryly observed, forget how we built the pyramids?

But if we think again, there appear to be many leaders. How about Steve Jobs at Apple, John Chambers at Cisco, and Bill Gates at Microsoft? Aren't (or weren't) they also leaders of the Internet? And what about the thousands of individuals who contribute? Isn't it more accurate to say the Internet is leader-full, rather than leaderless, and that leadership is shared? However it is characterized, it seems to be working very well. Meanwhile, we are left looking for new definitions of leadership.

Note an important distinction here. The Internet is a networked organization, not only in the physical sense, but also in its governance.

## About Visa

The answer to provocation 2 is Visa. In 2008, it was listed as the world's largest IPO until that time. The relevance for us is that Visa was, until then, a networked organization. Let's dig a little deeper.

Visa issues credit cards, right? Well, actually, it doesn't. Banks and other financial institutions issue the cards and provide the credit. Visa is a payment system.

Visa rose from the ashes of BankAmericard in the 1970s. Dee Hock, founder and visionary (according to the official Visa website[2]), led its recovery. "Visionary" certainly describes the way he organized Visa. It was set up as a cooperative run by regional boards. On these boards sat representatives of the owners (the local banks) who oversaw the services offered by Visa to its clients (also the local banks), who then did their own thing in customer recruitment and service. That's right. The same banks cooperated in the board room *and* competed in the marketplace. Few would argue that this sounds like a recipe for confusion. Indeed, the name for this design, "chaordic" (a word containing both "chaos" and "order"), implies this. However, Visa's record proves it was a remarkably successful recipe.

In his book *One From Many*, Hock argues that our institutions have failed us and need reshaping (and this was written well before the global financial crisis of 2008). He certainly reshaped Visa. Although he retired in 1984, the trajectory he set for it continued until 2007, when it restructured, and 2008, when it listed.

Why did Visa list? Curiously, it became a victim of its own success. The structure Hock adopted gave the appearance that banks could collude in the setting of fees across the system. This made them, as Visa's owners, vulnerable to charges of anticompetitive behavior. Reforming as a limited liability company offered better protection against such accusations. So Visa listed to antitrust-proof the organization. The IPO raised US$18 billion: the biggest in all history to that time. And to ease their pain, the owner-banks made attractive windfall profits from selling their portions.

A really interesting question has yet to be answered: Now that Visa's structure has changed, has it lost its magic? Time alone will tell. One employee said, "The IPO changed everything!"[3] and cited a new corporate jet as an example. The implication is this would never have been approved if the banks were still the owners. Another says, "Still happy to be at Visa," even though it is not "the same company it was a few years ago."[4] It would be surprising if new priorities did not emerge: Investors are now the owners, not the customers.

Back to our thesis: The design of Visa, a network, contributed to its remarkable success. Do the structures of the Internet and (the old) Visa share anything in common? How about these?

- Independent members
- Collaboration (and competition)
- Shared protocols

These characteristics echo our earlier descriptors: independence, community, and shared stuff.

The Internet and Visa have one more thing in common: Their structures receive very little attention despite their spectacular successes. To repeat: The Internet has no central governance organization. Leadership is shared among independent companies and advisors. Yet, or because of this, the Internet is robust in operation, and innovation flourishes. But from a management practice point of view, it's the elephant in the room that few talk about.

Much the same could be said of Visa. One of the few to remark on this normally unremarked-on fact is Peter Senge, who wrote in 2005,

Few even well-informed business leaders seem to recognize Visa as [one of?] the largest business organization[s] in the world . . . I have often wondered why this is so. How could [Visa] . . . be one of the world's best kept secrets?

   . . . Over the past decade, there have been well over a thousand feature articles in *Business Week*, *Fortune* and *Forbes* on Microsoft, over 350 on GE, and about 35 on Visa. I have come to conclude that the reasons for Visa's relative invisibility are as important as those for its success.[5]

And those reasons, he says, are in the organization design: a design that fosters the distribution of power and strategy. It is an organization that is "more like a democratic society than a business. If you are a journalist interested in the latest tale of business heroes or anti-heroes, Visa is the sleepy mid-west town of your profession." In other words, success on this scale is not newsworthy without a celebrity. And so to our third and last provocation.

## What Is TOYFNET?

I confess I asked you this question with my tongue firmly in my cheek. The odds are you have never heard of TOYFNET, which is our network. And unless you have used our product, there is no reason why you should have. We are certainly not in the same league as the Internet or Visa. TOYFNET[6] is important here because it provides the experience we draw on for this book. It reflects 20 years of learning, and it seems only fair to provide a brief sketch so you can understand our biases.

   TOYFNET stands for "Think on Your Feet® Network."[7] As of December 2010, it consists of about 300 people in 30 countries whose most obvious connection is that they all distribute a product called Think on Your Feet[8]—a training workshop (see resource 6). These workshops are sold and delivered by affiliates. Affiliates may be individuals or larger companies.

   I took up the rights to Think on Your Feet for Australia, New Zealand, and Asia in 1991. By 1993, we had 12 affiliates in Australia and New Zealand and a nascent network in Asia. Encouraged, we moved to Singapore for 5 years and expanded the network there, as well as in Hong Kong, Malaysia, Korea, Japan, China, and beyond. Success in Asia led to an invitation to set up the European network. So we moved to London in 1998. Since 2001, we have divided our lives between homes in Australia and Italy so as to support both the Asia-Pacific and European arms of TOYFNET.

It is fair to ask at this point, "Why did you choose the network option rather than engage employees?" The short answer is we didn't choose, or perhaps it chose us. Our reasons were very pragmatic:

1. We had no money to pay salaries.
2. I feared success. That deserves explanation. I was 50 at the time, and if we succeeded it might be difficult to retire, or so I imagined, with lots of employees. I have 17 years at IBM to thank (or blame) for that sense of responsibility. It sounds strange now, but then we were responsible for our people's continued gainful employment. IBM president Frank Cary once told me *his* challenge was akin to being the driver of a water-ski boat with 300,000 skiers hanging off the back and trying to turn corners without losing anyone.
3. I had no exposure to the networked organization model. My background as a school teacher for 3 years (equal parts public-sector bureaucracy and classroom excitement), at IBM (excellent training in a centrally managed economy), and briefly as managing director of Wilson Learning Australia left me with more traditional instincts.
4. My formal management training (IBM, Harvard Business School, the Australian Graduate School of Management, etc.) did not once invite me to think about networked organizations.

So I stumbled into recruiting self-employed agents and called the group a network. But this was with none of the awareness exhibited by Hock when he introduced the new structure at Visa. Even if I'd read his book then, I'm not sure it would have resonated with me.

But I was impressed by Sir Geoffrey Vickers who, at the end of a distinguished career, summed up his appreciative approach to business:

> I regard an appreciative system . . . as a work of art, both personal and social, one that is constantly revised or confirmed by three needs. First, it should correspond with reality sufficiently to guide action. Second, it should be sufficiently shared by our fellows to mediate communication. Third, it should be sufficiently acceptable to ourselves to make life bearable.[9]

I was attracted to the idea of a work of art acceptable to community, colleagues, and oneself. But I preferred the less pretentious notion of crafting. I was also attracted to the idea of an appreciative system as a learning organization. For example, the insight—at least to me—of the independence–community–shared stuff triumvirate came directly from a network meeting, as did a new appreciation of what this required of me as network sponsor. This led directly to my learning the new skills required to craft community—of which more, later.

The results have been rewarding. We have averaged over 10% growth for 20 years (see resource 6) and been profitable in each of them. We succeeded in helping many others craft the lives they wish to have. Ironically, I suspect we have helped more people continue in gainful employment than I ever could have at IBM. We have made many friends. We have crafted our own lives at the same time: spending the summer months in the Northern *and* Southern Hemispheres each year isn't so bad.

It has been an intellectual pursuit, too. I've developed a fascination with all kinds of topics—network science, complex adaptive systems, Visa, the Internet, alternative currencies, and more—that have yielded insights about the networked organization. This would only have been intellectual amusement if I had not been able to test these ideas, and the test bed is TOYFNET. TOYFNET is the prism through which I view networking practice and theory, and it offers the real-life examples that pepper this book.

In short, an uncertain start, a shortage of money and courage, an excellent product, an ambition to craft something worthwhile, and 20 years of practice are the backdrop for this book.

Enough of me: It's time to ask, "Who might *you*, the reader, be?"

## Who Is This Book For?

Who is this book for? It's for me, of course; it is a way to justify how I spent the past 20 years. But I hope it will also help others. I imagine you in one of the following categories (and I have been in each of them at some point):

- A leader of knowledge workers
- A network builder
- A network member

## A Leader of Knowledge Workers

You may be a leader of knowledge workers. You sense there are things you can do to change the culture, and you understand that the change probably starts with you. You are acutely aware of the advantage to you and staff of offering more engagement and better work-life balance.

Maybe you read Ricardo Semler's *Maverick*, about how he threw out the old rules, offered more independence, and allowed people to select their roles and bosses and suggest their own salaries.[10] You were impressed with the low 2% staff turnover he achieved and more so with the waiting list of 3,000 of Brazil's best and brightest waiting to join Semco. These figures say engagement and work-life balance to you. You sense (correctly) that Semler's design was network-like. But, you wonder, can these ideas be transplanted?

Or maybe you are simply aware that organizations full of knowledge workers are probably run by networks anyway. Have you have read *The Hidden Power of Social Networks: Understanding How Work Really Gets Done in Organizations?*[11] If so, you probably found the following diagrams as revealing as I do. They are both from the exploration and production division of a large petroleum company. They compare the formal organization chart (Figure 1.1)—the way many imagine work gets done—with the informal one (Figure 1.2)—the way work really gets done.[12]

Note the roles of two people:

- Jones, the most senior person, and presumably the person responsible for workplace communication, and
- Cole, one of the most junior people

Of course, working via networks has always been the case, to some extent: The old boys' network and "It's not what you know that counts, it's who you know" come to mind. But now there is another dynamic: the rise of the knowledge worker. Knowledge workers can't be supervised in the traditions of the shop floor, nor can their work be as prescriptive. They choose when and where to get the information they need. Finding the person best qualified to help—no matter where they are in the hierarchy—makes a lot of sense. It saves effort and gets better results, and the network diagrams reveal this. Now the maxim should read, "It's

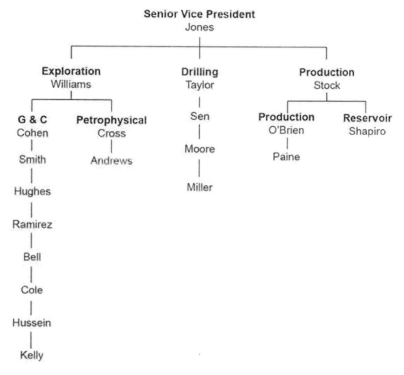

Figure 1.1. *The formal organization.*

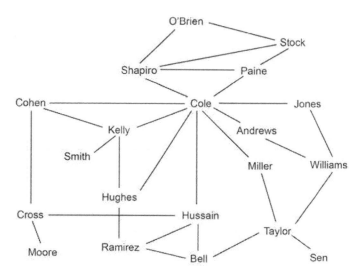

Figure 1.2. *The informal organization.*

not what you know that counts, it's who you know *because who you know determines what you know.*"

You suspect something like this happens at your company and that learning more about networked organizations might be insightful. Maybe leading *without* understanding the *real* organization is to be ill equipped.

### A Network Builder

You may be a network builder. You could be setting up your first network. You don't want to reinvent the wheel. You have many demands on your time and energy. Maybe you already have some neat service, intellectual property, or product and have proven it in local markets. Now you want to go national or international.

Or maybe you have been asked to convene a group of people who don't report to you. This could be an interest group, perhaps of clients, partners, and even academics, whose combined exchanges will help each other and your company. You cannot command seniority, expertise, or status as your right. You need ideas on how to host this pool of talent or community of practice.

### A Network Member

Finally, you might be a new member (of our network?), trying to make sense of why we do things the way we do. Or you may be considering joining (us?), and you want to know if we are compatible.

### So Is This Book for Everybody?

Not at all: If giving others the chance to do better is unappealing, then it's unlikely this is for you. (Don't get me wrong; there is plenty of scope for your personal success in a networked organization. But there is less scope for managing your superiority, however measured.) Or if the thought of sharing leadership is not attractive, then this book is unlikely to satisfy. Or if the idea of having to influence others rather than command them tests your patience too much, or if your shareholder-owners wouldn't allow a networked approach, then a traditional approach might be more comfortable.

But if you have decided to read on, here is a preview of what's to come.

# What Lies Ahead?

Chapter 2 offers the road map we wish we'd had when we started out. It surveys our journey from creating connections, through community building, to a coalition of peer networks. We hope this developmental model will be a useful guide to future explorers. And we tell the story of "Fitzy," a real-life participant, to add color to the model.

Chapter 3 flags our first waypoint: a simple hub-and-spoke network. But before setting out for this, we pause to examine the relationship between the network builder (or hub) and an affiliate. This relationship is the fundamental building block, and it differs significantly from the manager-employee relationship. This difference is key to the networked organization, and it confers a signature benefit, resilience, as this chapter explains.

Chapter 4 continues the journey. We add more connections to complete a phase 1 network. It asks the following questions:

- Why do we want affiliates?
- Who are we looking for?
- How do we find them?
- How do we select each other?
- What are the benefits when we succeed?

Chapter 5 moves us forward to phase 2, the crafting of a community. It shares our experience in doing this. It claims many benefits flow as a result, including, chief among them, shared leadership. Which raises another question: What, then, is the role of the hub or leader?

Chapter 6 attempts to answer this question. It talks about the new roles required of network leaders. Specifically, it suggests we require new leadership language, mind-sets, and behaviors.

Chapter 7 tells how, by chance, we found ourselves in the world of network-to-network networking with peers, what we now call a phase 3 network. As we became consciously competent at this, we discovered how it turbocharged our efforts. We then became more purposeful about it in ways this chapter describes.

Chapter 8 shows how easy it is to suffocate a network and draws lessons from an example; chapter 9 asks, "Who else has adopted a networked organizational model?" and offers some unusual answers; and chapter 10 gathers a group of friends in a closing circle for a final reflection.

Beyond these mainline chapters are six resource topics.

Resource 1 explores motivation, money, and alternative currencies. Autonomy is a reward and allows for other, personalized rewards. An expanded range of currencies enriches exchange and frees participants to craft the outcomes *they* value, including—but not limited to—money.

Resource 2 is a summary of what we look for in a new affiliate. It guides us in first conversations. We describe the output of a research project conducted with our immediate coalition of networks in resource 3. Resource 4 is a case study that invites the reader to design a networked organization based on the ideas in this book, and resource 5 is about network voice: how it is different from hierarchy voice, why it is important, and tips for maintaining it. Last, resource 6 offers, for the curious, more about our business, our product, and the contributors to this book.

## Takeaways From Chapter 1

- We state our central thesis: Networks are a potent organizational option characterized by independence, community, and shared stuff.
- To provoke our thinking we introduce two spectacularly successful examples: the Internet and Visa.
- It turns out that networked organizations offer surprising possibilities—resilience, innovation, and an abundance of leadership, to name three.
- However, networked organizations are largely unremarked on, perhaps for a lack of heroes.
- TOYFNET is introduced as the test bed for our ideas.
- We speculate about who might benefit from this book: leaders of knowledge workers, network founders, and network members.
- We are reminded that networks are the way work *really* gets done.
- We share a broad outline of this book as a journey from connections to community to coalitions.

Let's explore this road map in more detail.

# CHAPTER 2

# Road Map

Here is the road map for our upcoming journey. It takes the form of a model that we introduce shortly. We also introduce Fitzy and use his real-life journey to illustrate the otherwise abstract concepts.

We spoke earlier of Sir Geoffrey Vickers and his notion of an appreciative system—that is, one that is continually modified by experience to produce what he called a "work of art." Whether it is art or not is up to others to decide. But the following model was not in our minds when we started building TOYFNET in 1991. It is fashioned from hindsight or appreciation. It represents what we *would* have done had we foresight instead.

It describes three phases:

1. Creating *connections*
2. Crafting *community*
3. Convening a *coalition*

These are not neatly discrete phases. However, each is significantly different. A good metaphor is the phase changes that take place when an element or compound transforms from solid to liquid to gas. Think ice to water to steam: The constituent $H_2O$ molecules stay the same, but they exist in different relationships in each phase, governed by different rules. Boyle's law works for gases but is useless for solids. Consistent with our metaphor, each transition requires the investment of energy.

## Phase 1: Creating *Connections*

Phase 1 is the recruitment phase, namely, finding affiliates (individuals or companies) who wish to be our partners. Success in this phase produces a simple hub-and-spoke network as in Figure 2.1.

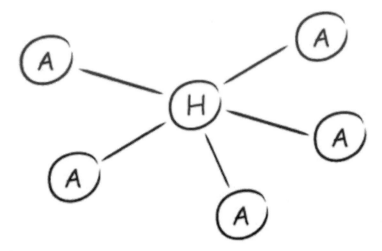

*Figure 2.1. A phase 1 network.*

For some network builders, the pinnacle of their ambition is to build such a network. We see it differently: This is only phase 1.

It is important to comment on the nature of these relationships. In the terms we shall use, the hub (H) connects with an affiliate (A) and vice versa; thus we see the relationship in Figure 2.2.

This is an elective relationship between two independent parties. It is the building block of a network. The horizontal depiction signifies the more equal nature of this relationship compared to the hierarchical (or vertical) relationship of a manager (M) and an employee (E) in a traditional organization as shown in Figure 2.3.

An affiliate's expectations are very different from an employee's. We explore this difference in chapter 3. Equally, the roles played by the hub and manager are different.

*Figure 2.2. The hub-affiliate relationship.*

*Figure 2.3. The manager-employee relationship.*

## Phase 2: Crafting Community

In time, we learned that a collection of H–A relationships has the potential to be a lot more, and the simple change (in theory) is to connect affiliates in a more thoughtful way.

This is phase 2, the crafting of community, and it yields the phase change depicted in Figure 2.4.

This phase has the potential for dramatically different outcomes. As community develops, so does innovation, collaboration, and the sharing

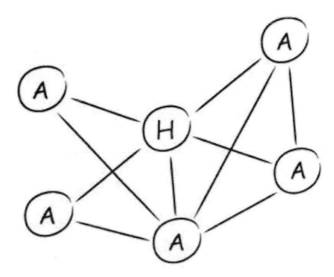

*Figure 2.4. A phase 2 network.*

of leadership. We talk about some of the surprising results we have experienced in chapter 5. To be an effective catalyst in this change, the hub needs to develop community-building skills (see chapter 6).

## Phase 3: Convening *Coalitions*

Phase 3 consists of a coalition of communities (or networks). We also call this network-to-network networking, or N2N. We engaged in this unconsciously at first via informal contact with other hubs in our industry, but when we saw how it could accelerate our joint development, we became more consciously competent at it. This phase, illustrated in Figure 2.5, connects hubs to other hubs and, often, their affiliates.

It is not difficult to imagine how this phase could expand into our ecosystem of global clients, marketing outlets, industry associations, research bodies, and more (see Figure 2.6).

These models provide the road map for our journey: from connections to community to coalitions. We differentiate each, tell what we learned about the transitions, and describe the benefits and challenges of each. From time to time we mention the science or perspective that informs each transition.

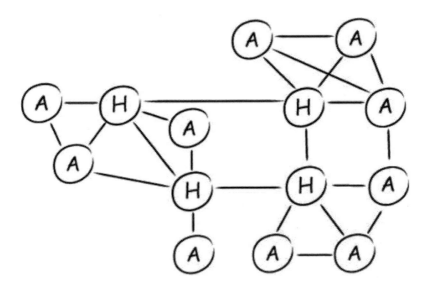

*Figure 2.5. A phase 3 network.*

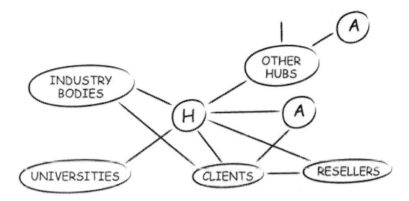

*Figure 2.6.  An extended phase 3 network.*

So much for the theory; how does it work in real life? To answer this question, I'd like to introduce you to Peter "Fitzy" Fitzmaurice and his story.

## From Tractor Driver to International Consultant

### Phase 1: Connecting With Fitzy

Fitzy was introduced by a mutual colleague. He had just left the State Electricity Commission of Victoria (SECV), in Australia, where he worked in human resources. He was looking for new challenges as a self-employed training consultant. He already had a reputation as a red-hot facilitator. He heard about us, we met, and he decided to add our product to his offerings. At the time we were starting out ourselves. We were delighted to meet someone like Fitzy. He had a good résumé, relevant skills (in training), and the right feel for the opportunity.

When I accredited him as an affiliate, we spent several days and evenings together in Canberra. A comfortable relationship developed. I saw him in action and became even more optimistic about our partnership.

Imagine my surprise when, a few weeks later, I discovered he was driving a tractor on his brother's farm. Why? In our innocence, we'd overlooked a couple of things. First, Fitzy's background in a bureaucratic, public-sector monopoly had not equipped him with finely honed marketing skills. Second, as he lived in rural Victoria, there weren't many prospective clients within driving distance.

We mulled this over and discussed solutions. I polished his marketing materials. He made it known that he was available. Previous suppliers to him at SECV, like Development Dimensions, engaged him as a master trainer. Our mutual colleague started to sell more than he could deliver, and the excess he subcontracted to Fitzy. The Australian Institute of Management in Victoria (AIMVic) offered him some work, and eventually, he persuaded them to offer our Think on Your Feet workshop. As his reputation grew, work came in, and we were both relieved that he was on his way.

Our connection strengthened naturally and rapidly. We shared an interest in creativity, and we both attended the Creative Education Foundation Conference at the State University of New York at Buffalo. We even thought about partnering in some new products together. We visited Philadelphia to investigate one such product. It was there we discovered a music club and a mutual taste for soul music. It turned out Fitzy is an enthusiastic guitar player of the kind of sing-along music I am partial to. This turned out to be a big thing in phase 2.

### Phase 2: Connecting to the Community

Network meetings had started by now, and a sense of community was emerging in the Australian and Asian networks. Fitzy facilitated one session for us and earned plaudits for his skills. Thereafter he carried the tag of the facilitator's facilitator. At one meeting in Singapore, he and I wrote words for a song to open the day's network meeting (to the tune of "Amazing Grace"). We rehearsed it in the taxi on the way to the meeting, much to the driver's amusement. We performed it 20 minutes later, with all but one joining in the chorus: Unfortunately, we had offended, temporarily, a dear colleague who took exception to our use of his favorite song in another context.

Fitzy's clients loved him. Some would use no one else, no matter what the topic. One pressured him to deliver negotiation skills. This was well within his capabilities, but he had no time to prepare materials. He turned to us and we contacted the network, asking if anyone could help. The next day Fitzy sent me an e-mail: "The network does provide. I have been overwhelmed with information and ideas." The mutual benefits of community were becoming clear.

Fitzy began regular international appearances. He joined our roster of facilitators at the Singapore Institute of Management (SIM). We taught together and coached each other. He became a master trainer and shepherded new affiliates through their apprenticeships (telling them about his tractor-driving days, of course).

Relationships develop in unexpected ways. A delicate moment arose when Fitzy taught for us in India. We got feedback to the effect that his wig was distracting. Did Fitzy really wear a wig? How should I pass on this feedback? I decided our relationship could handle such a delicate matter, and he confirmed his fine head of hair was all real!

### Phase 3: Connecting to Other Networks

In 1998, in a fitting irony, I was the one in trouble. I wasn't driving a tractor, however; that's hard to do in London, where I lived at the time. The problem? I could scarcely make an impression in the UK market. Fitzy came to my rescue. This was N2N networking before we even thought of calling it that, and it transformed our business. The connection Fitzy made for me with Monadnock P/L (a London-based training company) was just a taste of how powerful this kind of connection could be. Fitzy knew Monadnock via the de Bono network—the network that distributes *Six Thinking Hats* and other training programs written by Edward de Bono. Monadnock became our first successful UK affiliate, and we built from there. Monadnock no longer exists, but they introduced me to Ric White (our UK network leader and a contributor to this book), and Rob Fisher, a Monadnock sales manager who later founded Indigo, one of our biggest affiliates in Europe. And Ric, in turn, introduced other training companies he worked with as a subcontractor—like the Holst Group and Illumine.

The reciprocity continues: In 2005, our affiliate in Bangalore, Vicki, needed an expat to add to her team. She asked, "Do you know of anyone looking for excitement, challenge, and a modest salary?" We advertised this possibility in our network's e-mail newsletter, *E-NEWS*. I was amazed when Fitzy put his hand up. He had tons of work and a good income, but he was restless; his kids had grown up, and he was ready for another life challenge. The question on our mind, and his, was, how could he step away from so much success to take a salary comparable to one in India? We worked with Fitzy and Vicki to bridge the gap. We offered to continue using him on contract in Singapore, and Vicki allowed him time for that. Vicki got her expat; we kept our resource; Fitzy got his new challenge. All three parties were rather pleased with the results of this collaboration; we had arranged the first international transfer of an affiliate, something we'd never foreseen.

Fitzy continues to make a big impact in the region. Only last month we introduced him to a client in Kuwait. And here's the twist: In India, he is now in charge of business development. Not bad for the erstwhile tractor driver, now an international consultant.

Fitzy's story illustrates that behind the simple model we've outlined is a lot of life, experience, and color. It shows how we are independent of each other (we can go months without talking directly) yet how we are also interdependent. And while I had once shied away from taking responsibility for employees' futures, we've probably been of more help to affiliates in crafting their lives than I ever was as a corporate manager.

## Takeaways From Chapter 2

- We introduce a model-cum-roadmap for the book and for network building.
- We outline three phases. The outcome of phase 1 is connections, of phase 2 a community, and of phase 3 a coalition of networks.
- The metaphor of physical phase change captures the qualitative difference of each stage.
- We contrast the hub and affiliate relationship with the manager and employee relationship.
- We use Fitzy's story to illustrate what all this might look like in real life.
- A significant inference from Fitzy's story is that the hub and affiliate relationship need not be as thin as it appears to be: Independence doesn't have to mean neglect.

Indeed, as we will see in the next chapter, there are surprising benefits arising from such relationships: Specifically, we will see how resilient this model is in times of economic stress.

# CHAPTER 3

# Starting Conditions

"Some systems are very sensitive to their starting conditions, so that a tiny difference in the initial push causes big differences in where they end up," writes John Gribbin.[1] He continues, "There is feedback, so that what a system does affects its own behaviour"—an appreciative system, no doubt. In this chapter we will do the following:

- Note the hub-affiliate relationship as a key starting condition.
- Describe how this makes a big difference downstream.
- Show how resilience relates to autonomy, variety, and interconnectedness.
- Note why hubs might need to adapt their mind-sets to accommodate autonomy.

## The Hub-Affiliate Relationship as a Starting Condition

A key starting condition for a network is the nature of the relationship between the hub and affiliate. At first glance, this relationship might appear very similar to that between a manager and an employee. Some hubs would prefer that affiliates are indeed surrogate employees. In this view, affiliates are more affordable employee substitutes. This can be attractive because the employee world is familiar territory. Plus there is the appeal of (apparent) control.

However, many affiliates, in our experience, have moved from the employee role so as to enjoy more autonomy. "I'd like to see if I can make it on my own" is a common motivation. In this case, the desire for autonomy clashes with the surrogate-employee view. A relationship with this built-in tension is not a promising start. There are likely to be consequences downstream, and they may not be constructive.

All networks need some minimal hierarchy (and all hierarchies probably need some networks). So this is a not an either-or distinction we are making. But the openness of the network biases it in some interesting ways. One is the sensitivity Gribbin referred to and its ability to adapt as a result.

We started with affiliates because we couldn't afford employees and, because I didn't wish to feel responsible for their ongoing employment, we adopted a low-hierarchy approach. We didn't realize the significance of this then. In hindsight we see how this tiny difference made huge differences downstream. At least one of these differences made the networked organization a very attractive option.

The best way to illustrate this is in a real-life example.

## Surviving Pestilence, Terrorism, and Recession

The business lounge of the Grand Plaza Hotel, Singapore, is almost deserted. It's the evening of April 2, 2003. The lounge manager, Doreen, tries to look busy. The hotel's general manager, Scott, joins me for a cocktail. We know each other well. This is my 46th stay at the hotel.

Tonight, he is troubled. Severe acute respiratory syndrome (SARS) has hit. SARS first appeared around November 2002 in China. It has now spread across Asia. Travel has plummeted, as have hotel bookings. Scott's hotel is losing money hand over fist.

He faces a dilemma. Is it time to let staff go? If he does, he will lose experienced people and face the inevitability of finding and training replacements at some indeterminate point in the future. If he doesn't, the accounts will continue to hemorrhage red ink and the shareholders will become restless.

We speak softly. Doreen, one of his best employees, is close by. As it turns out, she is a mother of three who would happily take time off for a while if given the chance. But Scott has limited ability to offer individual packages. Any policy he adopts will have to be offered not only here in Singapore but also around the region as he is also the regional general manager.

Why am I here? The Singapore Institute of Management (SIM) is still running workshops, and I am due to start one the next morning. Empathizing with Scott's dilemma makes me wonder about the workshop. So

I call SIM and they confirm the workshop will run. I go out to dinner. When I return at 9 p.m. a message is waiting. The workshop has been canceled because of SARS. Now it is Scott's turn to empathize with *me* over the futility and cost of my trip to Singapore.

However, it transpires, there are more hazards on arrival back in Sydney. I suggest a meeting with my son and business partner, Peter. He prefers we meet by phone until the incubation period is over. Fair enough: I don't want to expose my grandchildren to possible infection. Thank goodness my wife takes me in. Some businessmen returning from China were asked by families to spend 10 days in a hotel. Then Michael calls to check if I still want to use his conference room next week. He clearly has reservations, so we ditch that idea. I am a social pariah for the next 10 days.

In addition to these minor inconveniences, SARS has a massive impact on our business. Revenue falls by 50% in some countries. We had not spent any time planning for this kind of event. Fortunately, our fixed overheads are low. But I worry about our affiliates. "How can we help them?" I ask Peter (by phone). He sensibly suggests I call some to see how they are coping. I do, and the results are surprising.

Elizabeth in Hong Kong says, "I think this is a God-given opportunity for me to refresh my spiritual life. I've been neglecting it because of so much work. I plan to spend the spare time I now have in prayer and reflection." That's unexpected but clearly satisfying for Elizabeth. She is coping very well, and she appreciates my call.

Andrew in Singapore is more pragmatic: "I've been so busy, Ken, that I am way behind. My website is out of date. My materials need revision. I have clients waiting for reports. I have plenty of things to do."

In Australia, a laid-back Malcolm puts it this way: "I guess I'll have to fly economy class and drink cask wine for a while."

I can't believe this good fortune. In the midst of a crisis, Scott's people wait apprehensively for someone else to decide their fate. Meanwhile, our affiliates are taking responsibility for their own lives, hunkering down productively until the storm passes, even though they have no idea how long this will take. Are we just lucky, or is there something in our business model that buffers us from external threats like SARS?

I begin to see that, yes, there are advantages in our model. The independence that affiliates enjoy, a fundamental quality of the relationship, means they immediately see it as their responsibility to respond. They respond based on what each values as the next-best use of their time and resources. These individual choices combine to give us systemic advantage. In short, we all survive by absorbing the pain in our own ways. For me, it reinforces that we should value and honor their autonomy. We should not see it is an obstruction; we should not try to exercise employer-like control because it would harm the business.

SARS is not a one-off occurrence. Since I started this business 20 years ago, we have survived the 1997 Asian currency crisis, September 11, SARS, and most recently the global financial crisis (not to mention tsunamis and the volcanic ash in Europe that cancelled our 2010 network meeting). That is, on the basis of our experience, we should *expect* a major, negative, external event every 5 years. Occurrences of this regularity ought to be part of strategic planning, and businesses should expect to have their sustainability stress-tested regularly.

As I write this in 2010, we need little reminder of just how major the present crisis is. Lest we forget, let me quote from *The Economist* online (December 17, 2009):

> *General Motors* went bust with debts of $172 billion, America's biggest-ever industrial failure. *Chrysler* also went bankrupt and was eventually rescued by Fiat. Other companies of note that went to the wall included *Nortel Networks*, a telecoms-equipment maker, *Reader's Digest*, *Six Flags*, an amusement-park operator, *Trump Entertainment*, a casino-owner in Atlantic City, the publisher of the *Chicago Sun-Times*, and *Waterford Wedgwood*, a maker of crystal and china.

The list goes on. I note this list doesn't include any of the financial institutions that disappeared.

An organizational design that improves sustainability must be a major plus, and our network seems to have it. The explanation for this resilience hinges on the *variety* of responses available across the system, and this is a direct result of a starting condition: the nature of the hub and affiliate relationship.

# Autonomy, Variety, and
# Interconnectedness Build Resilience

For this insight, I am indebted to Bernard Lietaer. Lietaer has been active in the domain of money systems for 30 years. At one time he was a senior executive at the Central Bank of Belgium. At another he was named by *BusinessWeek* as "the world's top currency trader" (1992).[2] He has written 14 books, including *The Future of Money*.[3] I was introduced to him and to the subject of alternative currencies by my German colleague, Roland Spinola (a contributor to this book). Lietaer says,

> A recent conceptual breakthrough, that takes its evidence from balanced, structurally sound, and highly functioning eco-systems now proves that *all* complex systems, including our monetary and financial ones, become structurally unstable whenever efficiency is *overemphasized* at the expense of diversity, interconnectivity and the crucial resilience they provide.[4]

In other words, diversity and interconnectivity are the building blocks of resilience. The Internet is a good example. It's not always efficient. E-mails might arrive in a matter of seconds or sometimes hours. The routing can be different and unpredictable for each message, depending on traffic and outages. But it is certainly robust.

Think back to our experience during SARS. Each affiliate responded in ways that made sense to them; that is diversity. Not all are individuals; some are companies with up to 100 employees. Nevertheless, in this diversity lies a previously unrecognized strength, resilience. At first, diversity may be perceived as negative—an inconvenient, messy, inefficient characteristic of networks: "I wish we had more control over these people." "Why can't we run the business exactly the same way everywhere?" "If only we could afford to own all these outlets, we could cut out overlap and make more money." That certainly would be more efficient but almost certainly less resilient.

Variety and self-organization turn out to be characteristics of sustainable systems. There is nothing wrong with efficiency—except to have too much of it. Too much introduces brittleness. When times are good, nothing is going wrong, and all the graphs go up, they go up faster in highly efficient systems. But when there is a crisis, they unwind even faster. There is a trade-off between efficiency and diversity that favors diversity, a trade-off that makes systems more forgiving, more flexible, more sustainable, and therefore more efficient in the long term. People running their own businesses tend to take the long view; it's their future. For them, bankruptcy would be grossly inefficient.

Let's return to Scott. His system is efficient. The hotel owners (bankers) make sure of that. Their preoccupations are occupancy, yield, and profitability—in other words, efficiency. But these are not balanced by measures of sustainability. He has few options; he does not enjoy the luxury of resilience as we do.

We *are* lucky. The decision to go via the network, made because we didn't have enough money to do otherwise, turned out to be fortuitous. It revealed an unexpected benefit of the networked organization model. We survived SARS and much more.

Let's return to the small difference in starting conditions that led to this major difference downstream. It resides in the fundamental building block of the network organization—the relationship between the hub and the affiliate (see Figure 3.1).

The horizontal depiction conveys equality, autonomy, and independence. We have a contract covering basic mutual obligations, but beyond that, we are independent. We own our own companies, offices, and equipment. We have our own sets of accounts. We work the hours of our own choosing. We take vacations, or not, as we decide. Most importantly, each of us independently determines his purpose, strategies, and business goals. And we decide individually on what to do in a downturn. This not only benefits the system but also is valued by the affiliates. As Daniel Pink explains, for cognitive workers, the science is clear. The desire to be self-directed is a primary motivator. It results in higher engagement.[5] That is consistent with our experience.

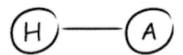

*Figure 3.1. The hub-affiliate relationship.*

Recall, for contrast, the manager-employee relationship (Figure 3.2). This relationship represents a hierarchy of power, control, and responsibility. This is reflected in title, salary, vacation allowance, performance reviews, quotas, office space, computer equipment, travel and entertainment guidelines, incentive plans, promotions, expectations about hours, dress, and spending limits, to name some. These are the levers of management. Taken together they order the life of the employee (and the manager). Add to that the expectation that purpose, strategy, and goals are determined by the top management, turned into subsidiary goals, and then cascaded down. It is clear there is a contrast to the hub-affiliate relationship and, in a downturn, very different options.

Of course, the employee might expect other benefits: financial security, access to tools, brand-name kudos, training, travel to exotic locations, and much more. And many organizations now allow—and even encourage—more relaxed behaviors like working from home and time for personal projects.

Some are innovative in releasing the levers of control. A novel example features the company Netflix. They have a Slideshare presentation about their corporate culture of responsibility. Within that, they refer to their vacation policy and tracking thus:

> Until 2004 we had the standard model of N days per year. Meanwhile we're all working online some nights and weekends, responding to emails at odd hours, and taking an afternoon now and then for personal time.

*Figure 3.2. The manager-employee relationship.*

An employee pointed out we don't track hours worked so why are we tracking days of vacation per year? We realized we should focus on what people get done, not how many days or hours are worked. Just as we don't have a 9 to 5 day policy, we don't need a vacation policy.

Netflix Vacation Policy and Tracking: There is no policy or tracking.[6]

And someone had added, "There is no clothing policy, but no one has come to work naked recently. Lesson: You don't need detailed policies for everything."[7]

That's quite an innovation and one difficult to emulate in countries where there are obligations for tracking accrued leave, I imagine. However, the gap in reality between hub-affiliate and manager-employee relationships is still wide. This new vacation policy was *ultimately* a policy—that is, it was decided on by senior management. In the networked organization, the hub does not even get involved in vacation policy.

## Why Hubs (and Affiliates) Might Need to Adapt Mind-Sets

Again, the different starting condition is the greater independence of the affiliate. This difference influences the whole relationship and governs the tone and content of interactions. However, both the hub and affiliate may bring to the relationship instincts finely honed in previous organizational life. Think back on the organizations you have been associated with as a child, a teenager, and an adult. What did they teach you about authority, obligation, control, money, time, the use of equipment, office politics, promotions, agendas, and the roles and obligations of leaders? Approaching the affiliate relationship with a worker-boss mentality can bring disappointment to both parties. Let me offer an example of each.

### Affiliate Preconceptions

Recently, one of our network-to-network (N2N) colleagues told of the affiliate who was worried about her income during the startup period. Helpfully, he thought, he offered her a monthly advance, and only an advance, until she got established. To his surprise, she rejected the offer, saying, "I can't accept that. It would feel like being an employee again!"

### Hub Preconceptions

For our first network meeting, I planned an agenda just as I'd been used to doing in my corporate days. Then when affiliates didn't agree with my emphases, I found myself getting upset. At one level I was thinking, how can we ever finish on time if people won't stick to the agenda? At another level, I was lost as to how to exercise control—as I thought the leader-boss was supposed to. Later, I reflected, what the heck? No good feeling that way in a meeting full of independent people. I suppose they also have a right to manage their own time, and it is their weekend after all. Finally, after experimenting with new formats that gave them more independence and control, I was able to say to myself, that's a lot easier, more fun, and more productive.

Therefore, once the new mind-set is clear, there is a path of acceptance that goes through stages like these:

1. I accept I can't be the boss like I used to be.
2. I need to reflect on what to do differently.
3. I can now see possibilities I never imagined before.

Ultimately, I came to embrace this: "How can I offer more autonomy than anyone expects?"

It also suggests why the experience we've had might one day help our clients, most of whom are more traditionally organized, and many of whom were our previous employers. While we sometimes call ourselves corporate refugees, we are not angry about our prior status. On the contrary, most of us are very grateful for what we learned at Ernst & Young, IBM, PricewaterhouseCoopers, Deloitte, American Express, GAP, Telstra, British Telecom, and so on. Maybe we can now help them in return.

## Takeaways From Chapter 3

- Small changes in starting conditions can have major consequences downstream.

- Downturns bring different challenges to a network and a traditional organization.
- Variety and interconnectedness in systems increase resilience.
- Networks with independent members enjoy resilience.
- Old mind-sets and instincts may need to be revised.
- Knowledge workers respond well when given autonomy.

In summary, the networked organization can exhibit unexpected qualities: Resilience is one. Any number of organizations would be happy to claim that during the recent financial crisis.

Now it is time to look closer at creating connections with more affiliates:

- Who are we looking for?
- How do we find them?
- What are the benefits when we succeed?

# CHAPTER 4

# Creating Connections

Let's now start network building, adding affiliates, and creating connections. By way of preparation, let's think about some obvious questions:

- Why do we want affiliates?
- Who are we looking for?
- How do we select each other?
- How will we find them?
- What can we do if it's not working out?
- What are the benefits we gain from a phase 1 network?

In terms of our model, we want to establish lots of hub-affiliate connections (see Figure 4.1). Together they will form a phase 1, or star, network (see Figure 4.2).

This looks deceptively easy. But it isn't, especially at the beginning when you have no track record. Later, with successful affiliates in place, you will have good references to offer and maybe enough income to make network building your primary focus. But this is a luxury at startup, when you will be simultaneously doing the following:

1. Generating revenue to sustain the business
2. Fine-tuning your product
3. Tweaking the business model

*Figure 4.1. The hub-affiliate relationship.*

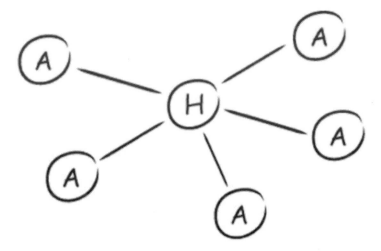

*Figure 4.2. A phase 1 network.*

Therefore it's smart to start in your home market. Here it is less complicated and less costly to hone your skills, prove your model, register trade names, and test contracts. Someone in a foreign market would be entitled to ask, "How many affiliates do you have back home?" Or worse, "Do you know about our withholding tax system here?" Or even worse still (as happened to an Australian colleague) you could be turned around at Heathrow immigration and sent home for carrying the wrong visa.

Having said this, if you get an invitation to start elsewhere, you'll probably take it. I did. Friends in New Zealand and Hong Kong sponsored my early client workshops, but I had worked in these markets before. But back to our questions.

## Why Do We Want Affiliates?

It's a good idea to be clear about why *you* want affiliates. My reasons follow. You will need to adapt these to your needs:

- *To grow faster.* Finding and training affiliates will slow you down at the very beginning—if you assume you would otherwise have been flat-out earning client revenue. So there is a trade-off for a while. But in the longer run, more people working with your products will generate more sales.

- *To open new markets.* Equally, if your ambitions are beyond your immediate home market, you will need local help. This also takes research, time, and funds but is also full (for me at least) of rich cross-cultural experiences.

- *To avoid borrowing or employment costs.* This is self-evident but important. At this early stage, borrowing to employ people might be a strain on the business. Or you may prefer not to be in debt—as is our preference. With affiliates in 30 countries, it was clear we could not afford to pay salaries in each of those. Nor would we want the costs of managing local employee-related obligations.

- *To add skills you don't have.* Language skills are the most obvious. But there are others—for example, the skills (and reputations) of local partners in their markets. A mix of industry backgrounds across the network improves access to different industry sectors.

- *To focus on the skills you enjoy using.* Most of us enjoy using our signature strengths and are most productive when doing so. Now that we are in charge of our lives, we can maximize our effectiveness. We can write our own job descriptions.

- *To build an asset.* A good affiliate network creates a steady, maybe growing, stream of income. This is an asset. Maybe you will wish to retire one day. It's possible a family member or business partner could take over then. Perhaps it can be sold—maybe to the network. These are good options to have.

Once you have clarified *your* desired outcomes, check to make sure you have thought beyond the obvious business priorities. For example, consider the following:

- What are your strengths?
- What would you rather do or not do?
- What are your family priorities?
- What season of your life are you in?

Three examples from network builders come to mind. The first returned from overseas to allow his midteen child to prepare for school graduation and beyond. The second went overseas in part to allow a very young child to acquire the mother's original language. In my case, I traveled extensively in my 60s opening up countries. In my 70s, I plan a period of consolidation, with my son, Peter, running the business. This is strategic planning on a life scale. This is a privilege enjoyed by few executives or companies. The normal rules do not apply. It's your network; it's your life. One privilege of being independent is to make it your personal work of art.[1]

Now that you have *your* list of reasons, it's OK to change them as things unfold. At least you will know the trade-offs.

## Who Are We Looking For?

We thought we were looking for just one type of affiliate—a person who is both a marketer and a trainer. So we prepared documents and processes for them. We weren't as well prepared for the other categories as they emerged. I guess the lessons are to (a) think ahead and (b) keep an open mind. We now have four loose categories:

1. *Affiliates.* This was the original and only category: people accredited to sell and/or deliver our workshops.
2. *Institutional partners.* These are associations and other bodies that specialize in offering open workshops.
3. *Intermediaries.* These are companies who outsource training services for their clients.
4. *Friends of the Think on Your Feet Network (TOYFNET).* This is a group of surprisingly helpful people.

More on each follows.

### Affiliates

Affiliates come in all sizes. An example of a smaller partner would be Triune in Singapore: Tan Thuan Kok (TK) had been a client at IBM before he took early retirement to start a family business with his son and daughter. Appropriately, they called the company Triune. Like other corporate refugees at the time, TK was attracted to Think on Your Feet (TOYF) as a way to help start his business. By and large, this group was very successful. Like TK, they took advantage of their prior management background and their contacts to establish a new style of work and personal life. It is not unusual for an affiliate like this to sell back to their previous employer. They are trusted, they know the culture, and they enjoy good access. Triune worked with IBM throughout Asia.

Over time, these family businesses evolve quite naturally. TK's son married and moved to the United States; his daughter started a family and then a new career. In time, TK retired or, more accurately, gave his time to mentoring. This evolution happened organically. Triune made sure all of its remaining clients were introduced to trusted colleagues. There were no loose ends: it was all very natural. There was no need for the intervention of a human resources department, severance packages, or hand-wringing over how to find replacements. People still contact TK for recommendations.

An example of a larger business would be Learning Masters International (LMI) in Japan: LMI employs around 40 people in three locations. I was on my sixth trip to Japan to find a partner when I reconnected with them. We had worked together at Wilson Learning. After careful evaluation of how Think on Your Feet would fit the Japanese market, they agreed to go ahead. We then waited 12 months for a slot in their development schedule. In all, it took more than 2 years from initial contact to revenue, but it was worth the wait.

One strength for me in all this was the fact my wife is Japanese. Her sister, a professional translator, prepared my first Japanese brochure. And we were able to pay respects to my mother-in-law while on business trips—another example of how networks, in their design, reflect the personality of the artist.

## Institutional Partners

These partners amplify our efforts. The good ones have strong brands, proven marketing approaches, and sound administration. We work with partners like these:

- Australian Institute of Management (AIM) in Melbourne, Sydney, and Brisbane
- New Zealand Institute of Management (NZIM) in Auckland, Wellington, and Christchurch
- Singapore Institute of Management (SIM)
- Capita Learning (formerly the Industrial Society) in London
- Hong Kong Management Association (HKMA)

You need to earn a place in their curriculum. At the very least, your workshop will need to attract attendees in sufficient numbers. Beyond that, bear the following in mind:

1. It takes more than a year to prove a workshop can be a genuine curriculum item.
2. This is a joint venture. We sometimes agree to share the profit and loss (or revenue) to signal our commitment to this.
3. They can greatly magnify your capabilities. For example, SIM's public relations department can arrange radio and television interviews. This is in addition to their press, mail, and electronic advertising. They can introduce you to sister organizations in other countries, like HKMA. The relationship with SIM has been in place for 18 years. We try very much to respect it.

## Intermediaries Who Outsource on Behalf of End Users

General Physics (GP) seems an unusual name for a company in training. Nevertheless, they represent a group of companies that will manage the business processes associated with learning and training on behalf of their clients.

A well-known high-tech company was a client of ours when they engaged GP, who became our new point of contact. We missed the direct client relationship at first, until we learned how to work through an intermediary. In time, this led to wider use of our products, in more countries, with the same client.

# Friends of TOYFNET

This is a catch-all category of other people sympathetic to us, our products, our purpose, and our network. It includes the following people:

- Keith Spicer, the originator of TOYF
- Thuan Kok, now that he is retired
- David, our first affiliate, who now retired but is still generous with advice
- Simon, a former client at PricewaterhouseCoopers, who has introduced several ex-colleagues as affiliates

These people are not active as affiliates but are of great value. We welcome them at network meetings and keep them informed via our e-mail newsletter, *E-NEWS*. They are part of our community (see chapter 5). They are a major asset of a special kind—social capital.

Several big companies now acknowledge the importance of this kind of group. IBM recently started the Greater IBM Network so ex-employees could stay connected.

These four categories offer our answer to the question "Who are we looking for?" What would yours be? The other part of this question is "What *kind* of people are we looking for?" For the affiliates, given our mutual independence, I reframe this question in the following section.

# How Do We Select Each Other?

For our part, we are looking for the following in a relationship:

- Trust
- Collaborative mind-set
- Relevant skills

Early in discussions we ask, "Would you like to know what we are looking for in an affiliate?" The answer is always yes. Then we state these as we did previously, discuss each in turn, and listen.

## Trust

If someone passes quickly by the trust criterion without comment, we'd note this and then use other ways to test it. We are trying to form an impression about values. My partner, Peter, has developed an ear (or an eye perhaps) for reading the materials potential affiliates make available. The words they use hint at their thinking. Take their website as an example. If it is full of (sometimes meaningless) platitudes used widely in the industry, if it makes claims that seem to be rather vague or unreasonably broad, if it lacks distinctiveness or personality, or if it doesn't reek of authenticity, these are reasons to wonder. And we reread their e-mails for the same signals.

Contrast this with the following example. First, Pascale and Françoise (France) had been introduced by a mutually trusted colleague. Second, their website and background looked really promising. Third, when I mentioned the trust criterion, they ran with the conversation for several minutes. They had both left Hewlett-Packard with plans to set up a boutique operation that allowed them to make a living, embrace their family obligations, and contribute to the community in which they lived. They had discussed values between themselves, at length, and were delighted to engage with us about trust.

You know it when you hear it, and experience tells us it's worth asking about.

## Collaborative Mind-Set

This mind-set tilts the affiliate's instincts in favor of cooperation and, thus, of community. It is not to be taken for granted: the default option for many in Western business culture is to be firmly competitive. This is evident in attitudes toward status, territory, or exclusivity, or simply a reticence to concede the sharing of space, even a space as large as, say, Africa.

On one occasion I was making a trip to a place much like Africa in size. I planned to run accreditation workshops for two people who lived 4 hours' flying time apart. I suggested we combine the events. It would be a richer experience for all concerned and much less expensive in time and money—savings we could all share. One resisted. He was concerned about the other stealing his clients. It took me 4 hours and three phone calls one weekend to reassure this person of the other's integrity and that his future would not be compromised by this small act of collaboration. He eventually accepted my assurances, and as almost always happens, the hypothetical concerns about poaching of clients didn't occur. As we shall see later, contact, and repeated contact (the so-called shadow of the future), is one way to ensure this *doesn't* happen. We make sure to connect new affiliates to existing ones.

Today, if we don't sense a collaborative mind-set and trust, we would prefer not to proceed. Our experience tells us things will not work out well for either of us.

### Relevant Skills

The relevant skills of selling and/or delivering are easier to talk about and evaluate. For our products, the most obvious skill is delivery. At the beginning, this is where we started. Before long, it became apparent that business development is the more important one. In chapter 2, we told how Fitzy was lucky to be able to fall back on tractor driving until he found a marketing partner. So if a candidate's primary skill is delivery, the next questions are "Do you have a good client list?" or "Do you have an association with someone who can sell?"

Given satisfaction on selling and delivery, there are two other criteria we insist on:

1. No one should decide until they have attended a workshop *as a participant* and are convinced they would be proud to offer it.
2. For anyone starting out in the business, there is the money test. We simply ask if they have enough money to survive for a year without any work. If this seems melodramatic, I point out they can easily spend 3 months getting themselves organized—getting accredited, running a pilot, setting up an office (even at home), organizing a website, developing marketing materials, registering a company, and so forth. Then it might take another 3 months to complete their first sale. (It took me longer when I moved to the United Kingdom.) If the workshop then takes place 3 months later, and the client pays after a leisurely 3 months (yes, it happens), then a year has passed.

So who are we looking for? We are looking for someone we can trust, with a collaborative mind-set, and relevant skills, who is proud to be associated with our offering, and who can survive the first year. (See resource 2.)

### What Is the Affiliate Looking For?

The affiliate is looking for the following:

- Clear information about costs, support, and accreditation
- Help—even if they don't realize it yet—in aspects of business they may not be expert in (Some accountants need sales help; some salespeople need accounting help. Sometimes the best thing we can do is introduce them to each other.)
- Product support (someone to talk to about technical and marketing issues)
- Assurances of independence
- The ability to craft their own lives (We ask where they want to be in, say, 5 years. One answer was "To be sitting outside my dacha in the country, looking at the lake, and drinking chardonnay." We have agreed to support this, and we are invited to share a glass of wine there. In return, we get help getting where we want to go, too.)

Much of this assistance we give up front, long before we receive any income from the affiliate. I liken this to the attention one gives to a newly sown lawn. It needs watering morning and evening to make a sure start. After that, it may well survive on its own: It is similar with an affiliate. This is an opportunity for us to make deposits of social capital.

## Where and How Do We Find Affiliates?

In finding affiliates, the early days are the hardest. You have no track record, no successes to point to, and no name in the market. You can only ask your preexisting networks for suggestions. In my case, these consisted of people from my prior work at IBM, Wilson Learning, my master's degree cohort, and my social life:

- Ex-colleagues
- Ex-employers
- Industry networks
- Clients
- Friends

Looking back I was very fortunate with help at this stage. Colin, a colleague at Wilson Learning and then manager of training at Hong Kong Telecom, sponsored a trial workshop and generously allowed me to invite contacts from places like PricewaterhouseCoopers and American Express. All became clients. John at Wilson Learning in Sydney offered the use of a seminar room, and I was able to invite him and my IBM colleagues (and my son and daughter and some other friends) to evaluate my new product. IBM became a client. In Melbourne, Charles, formerly of IBM, sponsored a workshop at a large insurance company. Terry, a management consultant in New Zealand (and also ex-IBM), introduced me to one of his clients, and so I got started there.

Why were these people so helpful? I guess they knew I would try to make sure they got what they wanted out of it, or I'd done something useful for them in the past, or I would try very hard to do so in the future. This is personal networking 101, I suppose, and it was hugely helpful in getting off the ground.

I did have one piece of luck: Having just left a senior position at IBM, I was for a while on the lists maintained by headhunters. I could not resist checking out some of the opportunities being offered. This meant I spoke to several CEOs. They turned out to be curious about why I was doing what I was doing and a few asked me to conduct workshops.

Later, when you have a presence, and the network has a good reputation, word of mouth informs your ecosystem. Eventually, a new affiliate attractor emerges: the attraction of a vibrant network. But to go truly global, it is still necessary to explore markets where no one has ever heard of you.

# How Do You Find Affiliates in Completely New Markets?

When I say completely new markets, I have in mind going into a new country—possibly one you have never entered before and where you may not speak the language. I shall give examples of how we did this. First, a brief diversion is appropriate.

## The Importance of Weak Ties

Try this thought experiment: You are looking for a new job. You decide to ask people you know. Are you better off asking your strong network or your weak network? (By strong I mean people you see often, at least once every 2 weeks.)

If you answered your strong network, the great majority of people agree with you, and I've asked several hundreds. It makes sense, doesn't it? The people in your strong network know you, understand your talents, and are disposed to help you.

But you'd be wrong. In a counterintuitive result, sociologist Mark Granovetter showed that consulting your *weak* network usually leads more quickly to a higher paying job.[2] Since his paper was published in the 1970s, it has been cited about 12,000 times. That's a lot of recognition from fellow academics.

But the really important question is, *why* is your weak network more effective? The answer is because your strong network adds little new information to what you already know. The likelihood is you share with them similar ideas, insights, and information. On the other hand, your weak network is a better source of novel information, in this case about job opportunities. It's this additional, unknown, and unexpected information that contains the real gems. Put this way, it makes more sense, doesn't it?

However, note that the definitions of weak and strong are somewhat arbitrary. Frequency isn't the only measure of the strength of relationships. Nevertheless, however blunt you might think Granovetter's measure of strong is, his result points to an insight that, when explained, makes sense. The lesson is to value your weak connections. Armed with his insight, we apply it, and it works for us. Thus we return to finding affiliates in new markets.

Before going to a new market, where we have few contacts, we consult everyone in our network of affiliates, and anyone we suspect has a link to this market, via an all-points bulletin (APB), telling them of our plans and asking for suggestions.

By APB, we mean the following: For example, imagine we plan a trip to Sweden. We ask our network of contacts if they know of anybody in Sweden who would be willing to talk to us: clients, colleagues, or even relatives. We don't ask them to nominate affiliates. Instead, we ask, "Do you know anybody who might be willing to have a chat over coffee with us? The purpose would be to learn about the local market. We won't try to sell to them."

When suggestions are offered, we contact the nominated person, mention the introduction, and ask if they would help us in our research. When we meet, we stick to this undertaking not to sell. We ask questions. We solicit information and advice. We explain just enough about our product so they can judge where it fits in the development curriculum. If they want to know more, we arrange to provide information at another time or in another way.

Here's an example that shows how strong weak networks can be. It starts in China, moves to Sweden, and then to Singapore, Poland, and Russia.

One afternoon, I called Jeremy Zhu Li in Shanghai. Jeremy heads our Chinese affiliate. I told him I was researching the market in Sweden. Did he know anyone at Celemi who might talk to me? (Celemi is a Malmo-based, Swedish designer of board games that teach business skills. Jeremy carries their products.) He agreed to contact Celemi and later gave me a name.

Some weeks later in Sweden I met Tore and Caroline from Celemi face to face. It turns out their focus was emerging markets. We swapped experiences about markets around the world, including Russia. I vividly recall their enthusiasm for this new market. I'd put off going there, feeling constrained by the difficulty of finding contacts, but after talking to them, I made a new resolve to get there one day.

Three years later I put out an APB asking for help in Russia. In Singapore, Tony, a colleague and client from PricewaterhouseCoopers, read my e-mail on his laptop while he was in hospital. He immediately asked his colleague, Susan, to connect me to Evgeniya, a Russian woman who had worked for them 2 years earlier. I phoned Evgeniya, now a vice president at a major insurance company in Moscow. She was nonetheless generous with her advice. It turned out she had once worked with Brian Hock of Hock Training. She suggested I contact him. She also agreed to meet me when I got to Moscow.

Then our Polish affiliate, Laura, responded, saying her colleague, John, was willing to travel to Moscow to assist me. John (an American) not only spoke Russian but also lived in Moscow at one time.

Pause for a moment here to reflect. I haven't even got my visa yet (and John told me how to do that), but I already have a warm introduction to Brian, an appointment with Evgeniya, and the offer of a guide. Thus one snowy Sunday night, John and I meet for the first time in Moscow to map out our week together.

We meet Brian first thing on Monday and ask his advice. He expresses interest in representing us. This is too easy: We'd planned this trip for 2 months. We have booked our hotel rooms for a week. We have 10 appointments lined up. And the first person we speak to is interested in representing us. Not only that, as an American who speaks our language, is married to a Russian, and has a successful business based in Moscow, he touches all the right bases.

I ask Brian to be patient. We then spend a fascinating week riding the Moscow underground and hitching rides (as many Muscovites use their cars as unofficial taxis). What a boon to have an insider to guide me. As it happens, John's weak network includes a headhunter who has placed several people into senior positions in Russian business, all of whom agree to meet us.

We didn't stop until the next Saturday morning when I met Brian again at 6 a.m. at Domodedovo airport. He'd returned only a few hours earlier from Kazakhstan. We reviewed his interest, agreed to work together, and shook hands. I don't normally expect a result on the first visit. (It took me six trips to Japan to find the right partner and as many to China.) I boarded the plane for Dubai. Few flights have been so enjoyable. There is great satisfaction in exploration like this, including the feeling of support from my crew—the network. It's not James Cook or Christopher Columbus stuff, but it's nonetheless very satisfying to venture into the unknown and succeed. At least, I feel that way.

But the real work had been done years before. The help we received from Jeremy in China, from Tore and Caroline in Sweden, from Tony and Susan in Singapore, and from Laura and John in Poland is what made the difference. All of them, according to Granovetter, are part of my weak network. I can only say it felt strong to me. Their assistance transformed me from a lone business tourist into a well-connected ambassador with a diary full of appointments. And what about Sweden? Well, if you know of anyone, we are still looking.

We started this story with Jeremy in China. But how did we meet *him*? This was via a special kind of weak connection we call the network-to-network-connection. See chapter 7 for more.

To summarize ways of finding affiliates, consider the following:

- People you know will help you if you have helped them or they suspect you will. This reputation, earned over years, makes a huge difference.
- People will help you if you are introduced by a trusted connection.
- People are more inclined to help you if they know you are not going to sell to them.
- Use your strong networks.
- Use your weak networks.
- Ask other networks' networks.
- Research online and in industry magazines about companies and associations.
- Ask clients: Would they recommend someone for you to talk to?
- Ask your country's export assistance office: Austrade helped me in Japan.
- Ask the target country's inbound trade office: The Singapore Economic Development Board helped me start there.
- Let it be known. Tell people you meet you'd be grateful for any suggestions.
- Be an ambassador for the product. Accept invitations to speak; you never know who might approach you.

And what hasn't worked for us?

- Advertising can generate inquiries but not the right ones in our case.
- Social networking sites, in which I have invested, have proved disappointing so far.

Finally, when you go to a new market, allow ample time for preparations. The 5 days of appointments we had arranged in Moscow took several weeks to set up. But also allow spaces in your schedule to follow up on suggestions you encounter. At the end of 5 days of searching in Singapore, it was suggested that I approach SIM. The meeting was squeezed in 3 hours before my flight took off. This meeting resulted in the 18-year relationship I spoke about earlier.

## What Can We Do If It's Not Working Out?

Do we ever need to end an affiliate relationship? Yes, although it is rare. And when we do, we try to do it naturally. By that I mean in a way that makes sense to both parties. When the parting comes, it should be as clear to the other as it is to you that it isn't going to work. Neither of you benefit from bruised reputations in the market.

So how do you make sure it's a reasonable parting? Here are three examples of increasing difficulty:

1. Sometimes the affiliate takes the initiative. One of our early UK affiliates, successful in his other business endeavors, never really got going with our products despite a huge investment of time and money. He wisely decided to refocus. To soften the blow, we offered his family the use of our house in Italy for their vacation. We parted on good terms.

2. On other occasions it's a joint conclusion. This can happen at the end of an accreditation session. We now make this easy by doing the following: We have a list of criteria we share with candidates at the beginning. We ask them if these are fair. If necessary, we negotiate these. We tell them we'll revisit this list at the end. When we do so, we ask them to rank themselves on a scale of 1 to 10 on how well they think they performed on each of the criteria we agreed on earlier. After the practice sessions and the feedback received from us and their fellow accreditees, no one gives themselves a 10. In most cases, we use this as a basis for planning how they will upgrade their skills *before* they run their first workshop. For a borderline case, this turns out to be a lot of work. As this becomes clear, it naturally leads to a conversation about whether it is worth it or not. A quiet chat,

and an offer to refund their money if they wish to withdraw, normally makes such partings palatable.

3. Finally, let's imagine it takes some time to resolve. For example, one of our best sales affiliates was prone to "red mist" syndrome. This phrase, borrowed from the sporting arena, speaks of what some will do to win in close situations. The player gets so excited he loses his cool. Driven salespeople sometimes exhibit a similar blinding need to win. They get so close to closing a deal that, tempted, they go a step too far. One began targeting the clients of other affiliates quite aggressively rather than developing his own. When we were told about this, we had a private chat about community and collaboration. When he later slipped up again, we asked him, "What should we do?" He asked for one more chance (which we wouldn't normally give at this point; but we did). He was a nice enough person but got overexcited once again in a bid to close a sale by casting doubts on the financial stability of a fellow affiliate. (You might be wondering how we know of these slip-ups. The clients told us, indirectly.) This last one led to censure by the local affiliate group. At this point, he volunteered to sever our connection. He collaborated in the orderly handover of his clients, and the local group responded by developing a set of collaboration guidelines together.

In our 20 years, these examples are rare—and rarer as we have refined our selection criteria. But they occur. They take a lot of time and effort. We try very hard to have them end naturally.

## What Are the Benefits We Gain From a Phase 1 Network?

When a functioning phase 1 network emerges, expect the following:

1. *Self-management.* Affiliates manage themselves. This frees us to spend our time focusing on their businesses with them.
2. *More reach.* More relationships with more affiliates adds network reach.
3. *Higher productivity.* Your efforts produce leverage.
4. *Use of strengths.* Do what you enjoy doing most and are best at.

5. *Synergy.* The chance to combine different strengths with others—a seller with a deliverer, for example.

6. *Resilience.* This increases across the business (see chapter 3).

7. *Freedom.* Both parties are free to craft their lives.

8. *Innovation.* Independence encourages creativity in marketing approaches.

9. *High motivation.* Incentives are built in when people run their own businesses. There is no need for artificial and potentially distorting incentives.

## Are There Disadvantages?

The most obvious disadvantages in choosing to build a network, compared to going it alone or employing staff, are investment, income, time, and control:

1. *Investment.* It costs money to travel, to prepare contracts, and to produce collateral materials. On the other hand, it also costs money to rent an office and so on, so this may not be clear cut.

2. *Income.* Selling and delivering your own workshops makes you more money, more quickly, at the beginning, so network building can reduce income in the short term. In reality, there is a lot of overlap: Every workshop is a platform for sensitively sharing your ambitions.

   But in the longer term, your income is shared with other entities: the affiliates. Therefore your top line is less than if all the income was billed through your entity only. In some countries, the top line is an accepted way of valuing your business, making this a real consideration. Whether or not it is more profitable is dependent on a number of factors.

3. *Time.* In the short term, network building costs time, as noted. Of course, it might ultimately mean you can retire with an income, so the horizon in mind makes a huge difference in evaluating this.

4. *Control.* "How can you control people who don't report to you?" is a question we used to get. For example, how can you control quality? On the surface, giving affiliates independence is an abdication of control and therefore responsibility.

This is an illusion, and quality is a good example. We need to remind ourselves that quality is a client perception, and the fundamental client expectation is reliability. The most basic part of this is that you turn up; that workshops actually take place as planned. It turns out that affiliates do turn up. And they do, despite flight delays, traffic problems, and health. It continues to amaze me that independent people never seem to get sick, or if they do, they still turn up. I have asked many times at our meetings, "Who missed a gig this year?" The normal answer is no one. I missed once in 20 years, but not for my health reasons. My son was seriously ill with malaria in China, and I chose to stay with him.

Once the affiliate has turned up, she knows the next gig depends on performance here and now. This is a great motivation to do well. Thus quality is almost never an issue. But the mechanism sustaining it is different. It's a different kind of control. Some equate this indirect control with being out of control, but this is misleading. As each affiliate is a manager in her own right, there are in fact more managers involved and therefore more control. Once we get used to the fact that control might not always be exercised by us, or in the way we used to do it as a traditional manager, we soon see *we* are more in control.

Today, there is a better understanding of the motivation of knowledge workers. Daniel Pink writes about what he calls "Motivation 3.0."[3] It consists of three elements: autonomy, mastery, and purpose. This is a research-based finding. The point in our example is how these all combine to prejudice performance in favor of high quality. So in theory as well as practice, most of the control questions about networks dissolve. Curiously, the debate has now shifted. Today, the question is "Why hold back performance (including quality) by exercising Motivation 2.0 controls—carrot and stick approaches—now that they have been shown to be flawed?" But this is not to say some hubs don't miss the comfort of control.

Thus in this chapter we've tried to answer these questions:

- Why do you want affiliates?
- Who are you looking for?
- How do you select each other?

- How do you find them?
- What can you do if it isn't working?
- What are the benefits when you succeed?

## Takeaways From Chapter 4

- Be clear on *your* reasons for building a network.
- Be clear on the criteria you will use to select candidates.
- Be open to more than one category of partner.
- Use your existing networks to get started, both strong and weak.
- Remember Granovetter and the strength of weak ties.
- Anticipate unanticipated benefits, such as high quality.
- Make any separations as natural as possible.
- Capitalize on your strengths.
- Allow personal agendas to guide your priorities.
- Craft the network that works for you and your affiliates.

Now that we have built a sound phase 1 (hub-and-spoke) network, what's next? From our road map, you will recall this is not the building: It is only the foundation. We now turn to phase 2: crafting community.

# CHAPTER 5

# Crafting Community

*Hundreds of research papers . . . point to the same conclusion. Human beings have an innate drive to be autonomous, self-determined, and connected to one another. And when that drive is liberated, people achieve more and live richer lives. (My emphasis)*

— Daniel Pink, *Drive*

Why craft community? To put it more bluntly, why complicate things? The short answer is our network said they wanted it well before we read Daniel Pink's book.

This chapter offers answers to the following questions:

- What is community?
- Why build it?
- How and when and where should community be built?
- What sustains it?
- What are the benefits?

We also share a story about how the crew took over the ship and sailed us to the edge of chaos and, ultimately, a very satisfying destination.

## What Is Community?

In our framework, community starts when the network moves from an unconnected to a connected state (or from phase 1 to phase 2). That is, it moves from that depicted in Figure 5.1 to that depicted in Figure 5.2.

However, simply connecting affiliates is only the beginning. Not until these connections have developed and deepened can we claim to have crafted community. A catalyst in this process is the discovery of shared stuff, and as we are connecting people who (a) embrace trust as a value, (b) are open to collaboration, and (c) are skilled in a similar, relevant way, that's a good start. Beyond that, they may share other stuff—maybe

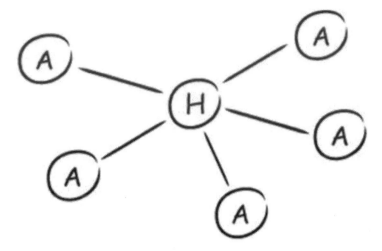

*Figure 5.1. An unconnected phase 1 network.*

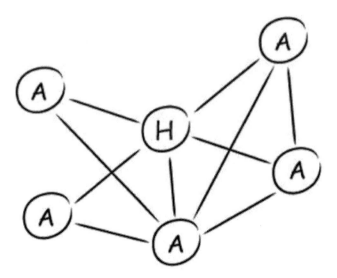

*Figure 5.2. A connected phase 2 network.*

a client, a specialty, or a common experience (including knowing the introducer). Then more value, which often derives from their differences, can emerge. These differences might be location, experience, or specific knowledge. In short, commonality builds comfort; difference offers opportunity. If in time synergy is realized, we see the emergence of strong community.

But it still starts with connecting. So the first rule is "Connect." And when we meet as a group, we have a process in mind we call *connect, converse, and collaborate.* If Figure 5.2 is the skeleton, the discovery of commonality, difference, and synergy adds the flesh.

Let me try to illustrate this with an example featuring Pascale and Françoise from Grenoble.

### How Connecting Leads to Community

Pascale and her business partner Françoise were introduced to us via the Barnes & Conti network in October 2003. I first met them by phone. This went well, and we agreed to proceed. Then followed an intense period of activity to help them to get started: I count over 100 e-mails, telephone calls, and other exchanges in the next 5 months before Ric arrived from the United Kingdom to conduct their accreditations in February 2004. Within another month, they make their first sale and they choose to invite Ric back to conduct it. The connections are thickening.

In October 2004, we have our first face-to-face meeting in Grenoble. In the autumnal sunshine we sit in Françoise's garden, looking up at the mountains soon to become ski resorts. We discuss their 5-year plan. Actually, we are really crafting a life plan. For example, Pascale was pregnant, so we discussed how the network could temporarily absorb some of her workload, if necessary.

In April 2005, I meet Pascale again, this time in Paris. We talk about extending the network to the French capital, and she introduces a candidate. I am amazed that this talented woman is back at work only a few weeks after her baby was born. Then in October that same year, they both join us with their husbands at our network meeting in Thailand. Here they meet other affiliates from around the world. Later that month, and now more aware of the reach of the network, Françoise accesses it for help. One of her clients is looking for a coach for a sales manager in Israel. We send out an all-points bulletin. By remarkable coincidence, a colleague from Sydney gives us a name that Françoise passes on. She later reports, "Thanks! My client just informed me she chose him as the coach for their sales manager. She is happy; the trust level is great. So I am happy, too!" We share this story in the network *E-NEWS* for everybody's benefit. It underscores the role trust plays in our network and in Françoise's client relationships. They are both becoming well known (and well connected) for all the right reasons.

In February 2006, Pascale goes to the United Kingdom to observe Ric conducting an accreditation session. She then becomes our France-based master trainer. During this session she meets Laura from Poland. Another strong connection is made. They meet again in August at TOYFNET 2006 in Brussels (discussed later in this chapter). In June 2007, Pascale attends TOYFNET 2007 in Toronto and connects with more people, notably the French-speaking, Montreal-based team. They subsequently collaborate on an updated version of the French-language materials that now suit both Canadian-French and native-French speakers. Fast-forward to January 2008: Domenico and Alessandra (our new Italian affiliates) travel to Grenoble to be accredited by Pascale. In the process, they learn much about the network over dinner with Pascale and Françoise, their very credible European neighbors. This is the kind of environment in which the network's DNA is transmitted.

This process is repeated over and over. The most recent example is piquant. Aviad, from Tel Aviv, is accredited by Pascale (and, of course, meets Françoise). It happens that both companies represent Barnes & Conti (via whom we met Françoise and Pascale), and they are both in the coaching business. That's lots of commonality. More than that, Aviad's company (N.E.W.S. Coaching) is building an affiliate network. Pascale and Françoise are now part of that network (as are, incidentally, Alessandra and Domenico in Italy).

I have just received a New Year's wish from France. It says, "Our special wish for you and us: Keep on developing our partnership in an innovative, elegant and pleasant way!" Note how naturally they talk about connections. If I asked you now to recount all of them, you couldn't. But If I asked you to reproduce the community diagram (Figure 5.3) you could do so easily.

Thus the diagram might be accurate, but it's shallow. It does not convey the richness and number of the relationships Pascale and Françoise enjoy. We need imagination to see beyond the stark lines to the humanity and depth they represent. Then add their other connections (the ones I haven't mentioned); multiply these for the other affiliates; imagine the

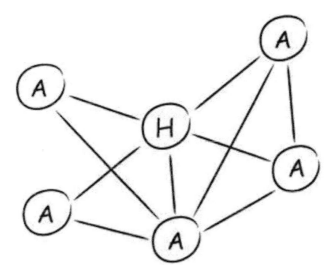

*Figure 5.3. A connected phase 2 network.*

nature of their encounters; add color, laughter, and music, and, hazily glimpsed, is my answer to "What is community?"

## Why Build Community?

What I want to focus on here is why we start building community. (Later I address the advantages we get from community, which adds more answers to this question.)

From the beginning I had a vague feeling that synergies could be realized via collaboration. But the *real* reason for our eventual community focus is because the affiliates said they wanted it. If your key business partners agree strongly about something like that, you'd better treat it seriously or start another business. To me, it's that clear.

A strong hint came over an informal dinner five of us had one evening. Fitzy was there, as was Judy (of whom more later). Fitzy announced he had a major opportunity with an open workshop provider. Unexpectedly, John (not his real name) said the person Fitzy was dealing with had behaved unprofessionally toward him (John) in the past. Hanging in the air was the question whether Fitzy should ignore this opportunity because of a slight to one of our group. I felt I ought to let this work its way through without imposing a view. I excused myself and said that I'd support whatever they decided. On my return, they said they would pass up this opportunity. I'm still not sure if we made the right decision—especially as it cost Fitzy. However, I was sure that it was right to allow the group to handle it.

But the clincher came during our first official network meeting in June 1993. It was a Saturday, at my home, in Sydney. We had a full agenda for the day, including the use of Grouputer—a tool Judy suggested. (Judy was a former IBM colleague.) The agenda ran late. By 5 p.m., the supposed finishing time, we still had not used Grouputer (a set of keyboards hooked up to a PC such that we could each simultaneously respond to questions). Judy had assembled this at no small inconvenience to herself: Recall the size of PCs in 1993? Frankly, I didn't think the exercise would yield anything. We gave it only 20 minutes during which we answered, individually, the questions she posed to us. These included the following:

- What do you value?
- What are your likes?
- What are your dislikes?
- How can the Think on Your Feet Network (TOYFNET)[1] help you?
- How can you help TOYFNET?

Then we went to dinner. Later, when I looked at the printout, it struck me. There, in black and white, they said they wanted independence, community, and shared values.

1. *Independence.* Most of us were at midlife. We had enjoyed the development opportunities our former employers had given us, but we no longer felt the need to be managed; indeed, there was a near-universal dislike of being bossed around. But more positively, we wanted to test ourselves to see if we could make it on our own.

2. *Community.* We shared a need for the company of like-minded others for sharing experiences, for asking questions, and for simply shooting the breeze with people who understood us and we could trust. We all had families to support, retirements to save for, and the normal obligations to mortgagers and the like. We were united in a

heady mixture of freedom, experimentation, and fear. We figured we had a better chance together than alone.

3. *Shared values*. In addition to independence and community as already noted, the most common words captured were "integrity," "trust," "honesty," "fairness," and "fun."

How could TOYFNET help them? They asked for professional development, a say in how many other affiliates were recruited in their area, and solutions to common problems facing small training businesses. Examples included "Which computer to buy?" (This was 1993.) "How do you keep accounts in this kind of business?" "Where can I find more good products to add to my offerings?"

How could they help TOYFNET? In return, they said they'd help us get where we wanted to get. Thus, if we could respect their independence, offer community, support group values, and help them craft their outcomes, they would happily help us craft ours. This was all revealed in 20 minutes, and in these 20 minutes, we offered only process and participated on the same terms. As I read the printout 18 years later, I realize they were offering us the terms for what people now call engagement.

These items eventually became our agenda as hub. We now say the purpose of our business is to help affiliates craft the lives they want. In return, they've helped us craft ours. Our product is the vehicle. Our business has not looked back from that point.

Now the learning starts: How do we do this? We are still finding out, but here are our current answers.

## How, When, and Where to Build Community

The first rule is to connect. Connecting affiliates requires a state of mind. Once you choose it, opportunities abound. And when do you do it? *All the time.* Sure, there are formal network meetings, and these are important. But before we turn to those, let's note the plethora of everyday opportunities that arise, many of which were mentioned in the Françoise and Pascale story.

*Informal Connecting*

Everyday opportunities to build community include the following:

1. *Accreditation sessions.* Attending such a session, usually with other new colleagues, is necessary to be able to deliver Think on Your Feet.
2. *Business travel.* For example, affiliates from Australia, United Kingdom, and Canada work at the Singapore Institute of Management. There they meet each other and local colleagues.
3. *Personal and holiday travel.* This includes traveling to and from places such as from Romania to Sydney, Guangzhou to Warsaw, Devon to Nova Scotia, and many more. All have happened. It's natural to meet up in, and even travel to, a friend's hometown when you are on vacation.
4. *Client premises.* It's surprising who you find facilitating in the next room.
5. *Meetings of other networks.* There is some cross-membership.
6. *The classroom.* Facilitating together for larger groups, or simply for fun and professional development, is encouraged—even if this means sharing fees.
7. *Special interest sessions.* One group met in Devon to do the cultural adaptation of a writing workshop from North America to the United Kingdom. Six of us holed up in a pub in Dartmoor. It was the only time I've ever had to disinfect my car tires, as it was during the outbreak of foot-and-mouth disease. The context often provides the shared memories that bind.
8. *Websites.* This includes a private site for sharing ideas and tips.
9. *E-news. TOYFNET E-NEWS* is an e-mail newsletter issued several times each year.
10. *Problem solving.* This includes Fitzy's negotiation materials, Françoise's coach in Tel Aviv, and so on.
11. *Introductions.* Every week, I write a few connecting e-mails in which I try to highlight commonality and opportunity, which go something like this:

To: Laurent, Caroline
Subject: May I introduce you?

Hello Laurent,
May I introduce Caroline?

Caroline works as a coach in Holland; her specialty is higher management–potential people. I mentioned N.E.W.S. to her, and she expressed an interest in learning more. And I know she will be in Lausanne on November 15–16.

Hello Caroline,
May I introduce Laurent?

He is responsible for the worldwide distribution of the N.E.W.S. methodology. Laurent is part of our informal N2N group. And he is based in Lausanne!

To you both:
I wish you productive discussions. There is no need to copy me on any further communication. One day, I'd love to know how this turned out. By the way, you share more than an interest in coaching: Both of you have dined at Casa Zazza!

Ciao,
Ken


### Formal Connecting via Network Meetings

Formal opportunities to build community include network meetings:

1. *Network minimeetings.* Janet is a founding member of our Hong Kong affiliate network. Sometimes, when I or someone else is visiting, she will contact the others, arrange a meeting and lunch at her club, and we will meet as a group.

   Lee Hiah does similarly in Singapore, as does Ric in London. On the last occasion there, we booked a private room in a restaurant. Unfortunately, it flooded the day before our meeting. At short notice, we changed to Green Park, where we hired deck chairs, sat in a circle, and shared gourmet picnic packs and conversation on a beautiful English summer evening: It was one of our most pleasant minimeetings out of more than 30 we've held over the years.

The agenda? *Connect, converse, and collaborate.* That is, start with introductions, offer a short briefing on product or network news, and then start a discussion. The World Café format works well. Small groups discussing something broad, like what they have learned about marketing in the last year, is enough to start an energetic and beneficial exchange.

And be alert to any other agendas. On one occasion, we needed to deal with a local red mist issue. The upshot was the group developed a set of collaboration guidelines.

Once you abandon a need to wow them with your PowerPoint presentation and decide instead to use the resources at hand, you quickly discover how much they will contribute.

2. *TOYFNET meetings.* A colleague from another network once asked me how I got people to come to our network meetings. Some networks try to mandate attendance. This sounds good in theory but is difficult in practice. If we did, it would be seen as contrary to the values we support—notably, independence. For the first two meetings, we seeded the process by offering indirect financial support (materials they would otherwise need to purchase). This amounted to 50% of their airfare. Later, the meetings developed their own attraction and momentum.

This leads to some guidelines for network meetings:

1. *Objective.* Design the meetings so affiliates want to come again.
2. *Values.* Honor independence and community.
3. *Process.* Connect the affiliates, allow them to converse, and wait for them to collaborate.

Here are some specifics:

- *Agenda.* Don't cram it with presentations. There is never enough time to tell the group about your latest ideas. Most of this can be done via video, online conferences, or in separate sessions before or after the network meeting.

  Even if your material is compelling to some, it will not be for others. They have paid good money to be there. They are independent. Find a format that gives you both what you want.

Our rule of thumb now for timing meetings is as follows:

- 50% of the time in Open Space,[2] or similar, led by the group for the group
- 35% in presentations and so forth (often without projectors)
- 15% in touring or cultural activities and generous breaks (apart from meals)

- *Action planning.* It is common in such meetings to spend a lot of effort agreeing actions to take afterward. Don't be too worried about this. A few key actions are good—but not a laundry list. This may disappoint those trained (as I was) that this is the expected output. Just remember that if you succeed in sparking collaboration, all kinds of constructive things can take place *in and after* the meeting. You don't have to force action plans through now.

  And there's another good reason for not emphasizing action planning. Our experience suggests few of these action plans get done. It's OK to rely on just-in-time collaboration. If you've been a successful catalyst for rich, new connections, just relax and wait. Connecting is the priority.

- *Process.* Adopt processes they can lead or comanage. Open Space works brilliantly for us. The World Café[3] works well, too. Kick these off, stand back, watch the conversations take off, note the smiles, hear the buzz, and enjoy the moving moments in the closing circle. In the meantime, participate or get out of the way. Offering a good process that they control is the best gift you can make.

- *Facilitation.* Invite one of the affiliates to lead the meeting. It is a great learning experience for everyone.

- *Connect.* Remember, this is your number one objective, and there are many ways to help people connect—generous breaks, for example. If you offer opportunities to see local sights, people will naturally team up on the bus. Some make appointments: "Can I sit next you between x and y?" At the destination, they talk while taking in the sights.

- *Circle.* Prefer the table group to the lecture-hall layout, and prefer the circle above all. What could be a clearer signal of community? It's the way tribes have met for eons, and a tribe is a good metaphor for a network.[4]

- *The outdoors.* Outside is preferable to inside (in the right circumstances), but a mix is good.
- *No projector.* I say this with a smile on my face. It's worth a try. Encourage people to communicate more naturally—as if in a coffee shop, for example.
- *Location.* Hotel conference rooms can be OK, but at least for our group, they tend to trigger default responses. It might be the smell of whiteboard marker pens.

  We've used comfortable buses or coaches, for example. One day we traveled around Sydney Harbour, stopping at picturesque places for sessions. We used the onboard PA system to continue the meeting while traveling. (Be careful though: We tried the same thing in Singapore and suffered terribly in the noonday sun.) We've also used a Tuscan villa, a yacht club, an island on the Great Barrier Reef, restored theaters, the National Library of Singapore, under a spreading oak, and our house. We even had a World Café session in our village's real coffee shop in Italy. Variety and novelty encourage people to come again. Location can be as strong an attractor as the agenda. Many people joined us in Japan because it was an easy way to approach a country they knew little about.
- *Have fun.* This is your life and theirs. Is there *any* reason it should not be fun?
- *Family attendance.* We mentioned that when Pascale and Françoise came to our Thailand meeting, they brought their husbands, too. Why not? Our businesses are part of our lives. Some partners have led sessions when they have a perspective we lack.

  The presence of children especially transforms the meeting. Here's a very personal example: My daughter Mariko, then five, walked through the living room of our Singapore apartment in her swimsuit on her way to the pool. In the room were 15 TOYFNET members just starting their meeting. Mariko noticed we were playing an introductory game using *her* jigsaw puzzle. She blurted out, with some hurt, "That's my puzzle!" (Stupidly, I'd not asked her permission.) John, trying to open the session, was nonplussed. Fortunately, Helen was up to the challenge. She thanked Mariko warmly for letting us use her puzzle, so warmly in fact that Mariko said, "Well, I've got lots of other games!" John was even more confused, so Helen intervened again: "Well, Mariko, why don't you bring out your games, and when we break for coffee, we will play. Is that OK?" A beaming Mariko abandoned ideas of swimming, changed, gathered her games, and then sat patiently on the side until break time, at which point Helen and several others got down on the floor and played snakes and ladders with her. (Maybe it's no coincidence Helen was later voted Singapore's Mother of the Year.)

Mariko stayed for 2 days. She not only made lifelong friends with her father's colleagues but also started to see what he did. More valuably, the mood of the meeting changed: Business people, on the floor playing games, connect at a different level. This, by the way, is captured in the Lego Serious Play offering for executives. There are other such stories. Make it clear: The family is invited, too. Allow space for them and observe the difference.

- *Fees*. We all pay our own travel and accommodation costs. We charge only for other direct costs, which we divide equally and invoice for afterward. This is helpful for their accounting. Claiming accommodation at a Great Barrier Reef island might tempt some authorities to question whether this was truly a business expense. Make any fee structure family friendly.

- *Giveaways*. There is no need for giveaways now. I've attended many meetings where a lot of thought has gone into preparing special pads, pens, bags, mementoes, and the other handouts common at such events. I have a cupboard full of them, and I realize we'd done much the same once. But our meetings work better now because the excitement, the entertainment, the fun, the moving moments—the really useful gifts—are within those present.

- *Values*. Above all, these meetings should reflect your group's values. If you believe in dialogue, in collaboration, in their independence, and in reducing the work-life divide, then these should be reflected in your meeting.

## Sailing Close to the Edge of Chaos

This story shows what can happen when you sow dangerous ideas within the community. The edge of chaos is the point at which a complex adaptive system (CAS) encounters unforeseen novelty. Some systems are complicated but not adaptive. Take an internal combustion engine. Its range of outcomes is very limited. It is not free to adapt or transform itself. An adaptive system is able to respond to novelty without losing its shape or direction. Many of the important systems in our lives are CAS. These include the stock markets, our brains, ecosystems, the Internet, democracies, and some organizations.

A networked organization with shared values and independent affiliates is a CAS ripe for adaptation at "the edge of chaos." This phrase frightens those concerned about loss of control. But it is a good place to be: neither out of control nor completely in control. The edge of chaos is where learning and innovation can happen if the underlying communication systems function effectively. The following story illustrates this. It starts in Thailand, moves to the United Kingdom, and then to Belgium.

At the pool bar of a hotel in Hua Hin, Thailand, four members of TOYFNET are relaxing in the afterglow of a just-concluded meeting. This meeting started with an exploration of values, self-organizing systems, and network science. Rebecca, or Beck as she is known, sits with the others as they wait for the bus to return them to Bangkok. She remarks that Peter (the organizer) is still running around like an overworked draft horse. All agree the work required for an event like this is a lot for one person. Beck pursues the thought: "Wouldn't it be great if the network took on more of this stuff?" Jacqueline agrees: "That would be Ken and Pete's dream."

Barely 4 months later, Beck is relaxing at The Swan Riverside, a pub in Lympstone, Devon, England. With her are Hywel, from Brussels, and Ric, a local. They have spent 2 days in an accreditation workshop. Someone remarks, "This is good. We should get together more often." At which point Beck recalls the Hua Hin exchange and says, "Well, why don't we organize a get-together of the European network?" Hywel suggests his home town as the location: "Brussels is the center of Europe." (He has just relocated from Singapore to Belgium. He is looking for products and people to work with. He senses that hosting this lunch-cum-discussion will quickly broaden his European connections.)

Ric agrees to find out how many Europeans are interested. When the numbers get to 12 in only 3 days and are still climbing, it's clear to him this will be more than a chat over lunch between a few friends. This response was not anticipated. Quite quickly the conditions have changed. Where will they all meet, eat, and stay? Who will fund the substantial hotel deposit? How will we manage the agenda? Who will lead it? Should we tell Ken? In sailing terms (as Ric is a sailor) they are sailing much faster than they imagined and the breeze is strengthening, despite a forecast to the contrary. Can they handle the boat well under these conditions with such a small crew? They are not out of control, but they are also not in complete control.

Ric calls me. I am surprised, delighted, and nonplussed. The reason for the latter is I'd agreed to go sailing in Croatia in the week they'd chosen. (I'm a sailor, too.) And if this had happened 10 years earlier, I might have thought, why didn't they check with me first? But I am relaxed about this now. It is a direct, if unexpected, consequence of our session in Thailand, which predicted this kind of innovative self-management and shared leadership. After an hour's reflection, I choose to cancel the sailing. It's not every day you get the chance to attend a meeting organized by your own network. I ask if we can also invite the affiliates from Asia-Pacific and North America. Ric agrees.

Peter steps in to support the funding and logistics, while Hywel continues searching for places to stay, meet, and eat, plus buses big enough to move us around and all the rest of the details involved in such an event. Ric thinks about the agenda. Eventually, he settles on Open Space Technology.

In the end, 35 turn up. The Open Space process stimulates educational, fun, and moving exchanges. I sit on the sidelines with a big smile on my face. This really is a great meeting. And I had little more to do than to turn up. Peter is more relaxed than in Thailand. Hywel makes seven trips to and from Brussels airport to collect people. Each takes an hour, during which he establishes a wonderful set of connections, many of whom use his services to this day, several years later—which underscores (a) the value of simply connecting and (b) that often the best things happen outside the conference arena.

Ric's standing in the group soars, as does his confidence in this role. The network becomes more richly connected. Powerful conversations take place. Collaborations ensue. We finish in a euphoric mood.

This was our first beginning-to-end event conceived of and conducted by the network for the network. Its success encouraged volunteers to host subsequent meetings—in Canada, Japan, and Romania. There is now a waiting list of affiliates willing to arrange and host TOYFNET meetings for us.

From Thailand, via the United Kingdom, to Belgium, this story is an example of how a network can adapt and innovate at the edge of chaos. Perhaps this is not such a threatening idea after all.

I said at the beginning that our first objective for these meetings was that affiliates would return subsequently. The question of whether people will come again leads directly to broader questions, like how does cooperation survive? Is there any theory to guide us?

### What Sustains Community?

Robert Axelrod framed a version of the question "What sustains community?" as follows: Under what conditions will independent people want to cooperate without the presence of a shared authority? The relevance of this to the networked organization is immediately apparent.

There are incentives for affiliates to cooperate—new information, for example. There are also incentives to compete—over a client, perhaps. This dilemma is similar to the one faced by players in the prisoner's dilemma, a popular way to explore cooperation and defection. Axelrod asked game theory experts to compete in an iterative, computer-based version of the prisoner's dilemma. *The Evolution of Co-operation* details his findings.[5] It is recommended reading for any network builder.

The winning strategy, time after time, was called "tit for tat." This strategy says that one should cooperate to start, reciprocate when offered, and defect when cooperation is not offered. Why did this strategy prove so robust? Axelrod's findings offer several insights:

- It pays to cooperate when the *gains* from so doing are thought to be larger than the *costs* of cooperating. So collaborative activities, like coming to a network meeting, must be more rewarding than not coming. Our test of whether participants will come again is relevant here.

- Cooperation can start when even only a minority engage. So encourage the opportunities that do emerge and then fan the flames. For example, when we reported to the network about Françoise's successful search for a coach in Israel, it signaled the benefits of cooperation.
- Once established, cooperation tends to increase, which is a reason to be optimistic about investing in collaboration. It's an asset that appreciates.
- If it comes to be adopted by virtually everyone, then (a) individuals can afford to be generous, and (b) the group can protect itself against individuals who defect (as in the example of the affiliate with red mist syndrome).
- The shadow of the future (i.e., the likelihood of future encounters) cements cooperation. Therefore it's helpful to support the expectation of regular, future encounters and to ensure they happen.

In short, the community remembers. It rewards cooperation and punishes defection. It has a life of its own. This is a provocative and encouraging finding. Now let's turn to our last question.

## What Are the Benefits of Community?

Some (not many) have suggested it might be better to keep affiliates apart, or at least not to actively encourage community. There are a few reasons for this. The first is the cost. It requires an investment of energy, time, and money. The second is a concern that this new organism might have a life of its own (which it will) and that this life might not be in a form that is easy to control. It might even take the form of a pressure group. This concern is real *if* hub-to-affiliate relationships are in disrepair. However, our experience is that crafting community offers handsome returns on our investment. Here are the key ones:

- *Shared leadership and multiple leaders.* This must be the stand-out benefit. Recall the Brussels meeting. Multiply this many times over and the result is a leader-full organization. Many organizations struggle to find or develop leaders and spend enormous amounts doing so. With a view that anyone can be a leader, what emerges are reserves of leadership available to the whole community.

- *Innovation.* Harvesting the network is the easy way to reap product development ideas. It's also a source of breakthroughs in marketing and production that can be shared.
- *Solace.* There is nothing like a group of like-minded friends within which to find comfort, conversation, and consolation when necessary.
- *Resources.* If you are short of something, you can turn to the network. Laura in Poland had more work than she could handle at one point. She was forced to decide about which client to disappoint—until, that is, she thought to ask Beck if she'd like a trip to Warsaw. Problem solved. Laura's clients were happy. Laura increased her company's workforce for one week and got the revenue. Beck and her husband saw the sights of Warsaw.
- *Work.* As Hywel found out, the community is a great place to meet those who want to use your services.
- *Experience.* Someone, somewhere has likely solved your problem before. If you can meet them, all benefit.
- *Fun.* James, from China, met Laura (Poland) at a network meeting. Later, he stayed with her family on his vacation. What's more, as she was working, he went to observe, to help and to learn. It was a busman's holiday, indeed, and a lasting cross-cultural friendship.
- *Growth.* Like-minded people are a good source of new product suggestions.
- *A de facto organization.* We gain a de facto organization without the overheads of a normal organization. It is an organization funded by social, rather than financial, capital. If its reputation is good, it attracts more affiliates.

# Takeaways From Chapter 5

- Affiliates want community *and* independence.
- If we help them craft their lives, they will reciprocate.
- Community is founded on commonality and developed via difference.
- Formal meetings—short and long—play a role.
- Use meeting processes that allow affiliates to connect, converse, and collaborate.
- The edge of chaos is a good place to be if network communications are good.
- Cooperation can survive and thrive even in a hostile environment.
- Communities can be leader-full.
- A sound community, founded on social capital, is an organization for free.
- A good community attracts more members.

We now face another question: if the hub is the counterpart to the leader in a traditional organization, how does he exercise leadership in a community? This is the subject of our next chapter.

# CHAPTER 6

# Hosting as Leading

The question now is, what is the role of the hub? Literature, politics, and popular culture have established the heroic leader as a stereotype. But a search for better models is under way. I propose to put a case here for the leader as host, at least when the leader is the hub of a network. I will suggest what the hub hosts, speculate on other emerging metaphors, and offer a thought experiment to explore these ideas.

## The Stereotype

It starts with the language of leadership and its origins. From the military we get words like *officer, strategy, target, territory, promotion, headquarters, staff, line,* and *division.* How these commanding words have been absorbed into popular culture is nicely illustrated by a magazine advertisement I read today.[1] It featured "The Leader's Watch," a new model with a "more commanding" size. Leadership, command, and size are words that go easily together in the heroic model. (And CEOs are significantly taller than average, as a group, which shows either how size matters or how we discriminate unfairly against talented shorter executives and therefore need a more inclusive language.[2])

Now consider words from the church, like *mission, vision, followers, inspiration, hierarchy,* and *beliefs,* as well as words from mechanics, with *reengineering, leverage,* and *scientific management.* And don't forget sports, with *team, competition, players, fitness,* and *level playing field,* and we cover much of the management lexicon.

But this view of leading is *misleading.* On the one hand, we don't consider Gandhi or Mandela commanding in the military sense and clearly not wearing a larger watch as a power accessory. Certainly, in our more modest situation as a network hub trying to craft community, it is not immediately obvious where or how the heroic posture fits.

In my view we need a new, or at least expanded, language and view of leadership.

## The Debate

Dee Hock (of Visa fame) was convinced the command-and-control model of organization was a leftover from the industrial revolution, "archaic and increasingly irrelevant."[3] He eschewed military and mechanical models in favor of biological ones, which allow an organization to "evolve [and] . . . to invent and organize itself . . . like the body, the brain and the biosphere."[4] Once these concepts and ideas take root, such organizations should be "management proof,"[5] he said.

Hock thought the idea of the irreplaceable leader was nonsense as long as the right organizational design was in place. In this case, the place would be full of leaders. He backed his own convictions and retired from Visa in 1984 giving only 3 months' notice. Contrary to predictions, Visa continued to outperform others in its industry for long after that.

Ricardo Semler of Semco, after collapsing (literally) under the load of leadership, decided to let go in favor of his employees running more of the business. He discovered that "the more freedom he gave his staff to set their own schedules, the more versatile, productive and loyal they became, and the better Semco performed."[6]

Peter Block calls for us to "deglamorize leadership and consider it a quality that exists in all human beings."[7] He is my source of the host metaphor.

Alfie Kohn in 1993 argued that using incentives doesn't make sense.[8] As Daniel Pink recently added, these are merely instruments of control and remnants of a mechanical view of management (if this, then that).[9] He shows that, no matter how counterintuitive it sounds, incentives are likely to impair performance—except when the work is inherently uninteresting. He suggests we focus on the things that motivate people like those in our network, namely, autonomy, mastery, and purpose. His metaphor for management thinking is software, and it needs upgrading. If Motivation 1.0 was about survival, and Motivation 2.0 is about extrinsic rewards, we need to move to Motivation 3.0, which is about intrinsic rewards.

Professor Bob Sutton of Stanford Business School spoke recently in a video about the leader or manager as a gardener, another metaphor I like.[10] A gardener presumably plants seeds, nurtures them, and encourages growth. In some places, this would literally be a life-saving change. In "Why Good Bosses Tune In to Their People," he writes, "Lousy bosses can kill you—literally. A 2009 Swedish study tracking 3,122 men for ten years found those with bad bosses suffered 20 to 40 percent more heart attacks than those with good bosses."[11] But then his message gets confused when he says that "good bosses . . . project power" and follows up with seven "Tricks for Taking Charge," summarized here:

1. Talk more than others but not the whole time.
2. Interrupt occasionally and don't let others interrupt you too much.
3. Cross your arms when you talk.
4. Use positive self-talk.
5. Try a flash of anger occasionally.
6. If you aren't sure whether to sit or to stand, stand.
7. Surrender some power or status but make sure everyone knows that you did so freely.

These displays of strength and privilege (presumably employees aren't supposed to use these tricks) don't sound like gardening or tuning in to people. I might be doing Professor Sutton a disservice, but my concern is for the students who will be the next generation of leaders. Maybe we are just confused and still working it out. Are we between trapezes, so to speak, stretching for a new model but scared to let go of the old one?

Against this backdrop, and with the role of network hub in mind, let me explain why the hub (or leader) as host appeals.

## The Hub as Host

In May 2008 I attended a session led by Peter Block called "Community: The Structure of Belonging." In this session he put forward the case for the leader as host. It hit me immediately as being right for hubs.

It resonated deeply because it encompassed the things we talked about in the last chapter on community. And it felt comfortable. I've never been comfortable with the idea of a commanding leader. But I feel no immodesty in saying we are good hosts. This plays to our strengths. It frees us to be natural. Block highlighted what he called some truths about leaders and hosting:[12]

- The core task of leaders is to build community.
- Trust is the basis of community.
- Effective community underpins performance.
- Leaders should learn how to convene; it's too important to be left to trained specialists.
- Conversation, around the right questions, allows the community to become competent.
- How we gather matters: For example, the circle trumps the rectangle, and the auditorium ought to be used only for performances.

Notice the words in common with those I used in only the last chapter: *community, trust, performance, conversation*, and *circle*. The things we'd learned quite slowly were summed up in this metaphor. If only we'd had Block's insight earlier.

## What Does the Hub Host?

I suggest hubs are hosts of the following:

1. Conversations
2. Ambitions
3. Meaning

### *Hosting Conversations*

What words do you associate with "host" and "hosting"? The role of the host at a meal fits well. She issues invitations, organizes the space, introduces people, and seeds conversation. These are all parallels for activities we've described earlier.

And it's more than a metaphor. In reality, much of our business *is* done over coffee, lunch, or dinner and not infrequently at home. We sometimes talk about meeting over "breakfast at Balmoral" for exchanges. Balmoral is a beach in Sydney near where I live, but the metaphor is meant to cover any location where the same atmosphere exists. When I want to meet people in Sydney, I say, "Shall we meet in your office, or my home office, or at Balmoral?" Overwhelmingly, people choose the latter. Then we decide if we'll walk along the beach, have coffee, a meal, or any combination. Then we meet and talk about anything we like—often including business. Hosting is nearly perfect for the way we run our meetings, too. It's no accident that we adopt processes like the World Café to trigger the openness and spontaneity of the coffee shop. And since the network has started hosting our meetings, they seem very comfortable returning the hospitality. That is, hosting works well with shared leadership.

Hosting is central to the crafting of community. It encompasses our core processes: connecting, conversing, and collaborating.

### Hosting Ambitions

We are also hosts to affiliate ambitions. Take, as an example, helping Fitzy craft a life change. Hosting ambitions also have a more prosaic side in everyday problem solving. Peter, who is our CEO, describes himself as a professional problem solver. In his terms, a problem is the difference between where someone is and where they want to be. Clearly, this covers the expected, like arranging an urgent shipment. But it goes further. If Jeremy (in China) is searching for products in the area of change management, Peter will help him them find these, too.

Prosaic problems or grand ambitions are equally covered by the hosting role. They all fall within our role (or perhaps our mission) of helping affiliates to craft their desired futures.

### Hosting Meaning

Hosting also means acting as a custodian of meaning. I acknowledge the insight of David Limerick and Bert Cunnington for this.[13] Like Block's hosting insight, it resonated for me as I read it. Their synthesis (written in 1993) predicted a future of economic uncertainty, loosely coupled organizations, synergies, alliances via networks, collaborative individualism, and *the importance of managing meaning*. From my perspective 20 years later, they were spot on.

Although the idea of manager of meaning struck me, I prefer the role of custodian. But we mean the same. As they say, "What keeps the organization together is a field of shared values, goals and beliefs."[14] Presumably, then, if these are not preserved, the organization risks disintegration. (See chapter 8.)

You might recall our first network meeting in 1993 at which the Grouputer exercise highlighted group values, goals, and beliefs. I described this as shared stuff. When I later read Limerick and Cunnington, they helped me see my role as custodian of the shared stuff. Today, this stuff includes many things: the product, its value, its well-being and reputation, delivery, protection, and reputation, as well as the core values of trust, integrity, independence, and community.

Since then we have focused on, and experimented with, ways to fulfill this role. Some attempts made no impact. Others seemed to work, judged by feedback from the network. They included the following:

- *Prisoner's dilemma.* We played this and debriefed what it meant for collaboration.
- *Reporting.* We present our financial results to the network. We hope to show we have nothing to hide and to promote openness.
- *Collaboration guidelines.* We developed these together after the red mist incidents, as group-devised guidelines for those sharing markets.
- *Deep Simplicity.* In Thailand, Ric, Jacqueline, and I ran a workshop that focused on self-organization, complexity, and shared leadership. This was the first time we shared some of these ideas with the network.
- *BOIDS.* This exercise was conducted first in Thailand and subsequently in other meetings. (It is described in the thought experiment later in this chapter.)

The feedback was clear. When Beck said, after Deep Simplicity, "Now I get where you're coming from," I wished we'd started much earlier. Then she sent me a book on the subject.

What held us back? Was it our or my preconceptions about leadership? Thomas Power (chairman of Ecademy) says it took him 10 years to make the mind shift from "institutional thinking—closed, selective, controlling" to "network thinking—open, random, supportive."[15] He has a point. I doubt the Facebook generation will take as long.

While talking about what *we* did, I should emphasize the role played by affiliates in being co-custodians of meaning. Mary in Singapore wrote at one point to Jeremy and a large client in China. The client had used her in Singapore and now wanted to run our program in China. Mary wrote, "In our world-wide network we link people and needs. This is the privilege of being part of the world's greatest network." Allowing for some hyperbole, the network shares a view of what we are about and transmits this in their words. Ideas take on a life of their own; they become memes.

"Memes" is a term introduced by Richard Dawkins in *The Selfish Gene* to describe ideas, concepts, and techniques that, in a manner analogous to genes, take on an existence of their own.[16] For memes, think melodies, catchphrases, fashions, techniques, concepts of leadership, and so on that are transmitted, mutated, culturally embellished, and compete with each other. When Mary chose to say what she did, she transmitted memes about the Think on Your Feet Network (TOYFNET) to a colleague and a client.

What else does the host as custodian of memes do? She pays attention, notices, and reflects back to the network. For example, when the network solved Françoise's need for a coach in Israel, we issued an *E-NEWS*. This gave a chance to reflect on (a) the strength of weak connections, (b) how TOYFNET is a conduit to these, (c) how this multiplies everybody's social equity, and ultimately (d) how this improves business performance. Network membership grows in value, too.

All of these attentions add up to being a custodian of meaning. And as Limerick and Cunnington said, this shared stuff becomes the organizational glue. In summary, the hub—as host—hosts conversations, ambitions, and meaning.

## New Metaphors

If military, missionary, and mechanical metaphors were better suited for the industrial revolution, as Hock suggests, with what shall we replace them? As a pointer, Stanley Davis says the natural progression is a good starting point.[17] By natural progression he means from the universe to science to technology to product to organization—with the latter always playing catch-up.

One example of such a progression would be from gravity (the universe), to Newton's mechanics (science), to machines (technology), to cars (products), to mass production and Sloan's organizational models at GM, famously publicized by Peter Drucker and still the basis of much management practice. The mechanical practice of management was in stark contrast to today's needs, if Sloan's competitor Henry Ford was any guide. He said, "The average worker wants a job . . . in which he does not have to think. Why is it when I ask for a pair of hands a brain comes attached?"[18]

If we accept this idea that the windows of science might offer a glimpse of organizational possibilities, we are led to new metaphors. Biological metaphors are popular and informative: They include evolution, niches, genetics (memes), ecosystems, the brain, natural organizations, and gardening.

Quantum physics offers others. In *Leadership and the New Science*, Margaret Wheatley traces a progression from the new science (quantum physics), to the transistor, to the computer, to complex systems, to the potential for physical and human systems to self-organize.[19] And as already noted, Pink uses a computer operating system as a way to explore new management thinking.

One emerging new area of science is network science. It spans both mathematics and sociology and is already influencing thinking about organizations.

But for now, let's look more closely at a metaphor called BOIDS. BOIDS is how a New Yorker might say "birds." Some birds flock in complexly coordinated movements. How do they do this without crashing into each other? Craig Reynolds built a computer model to explore this.[20] He was able to show that birds (or BOIDS) could flock by following three simple rules:

1. *Separation.* Steer to avoid crowding nearby flockmates.
2. *Alignment.* Steer toward the average heading of local flockmates.
3. *Cohesion.* Steer to move toward the average position of local flockmates.

It's not a big leap from separation, alignment, and cohesion to independence, shared stuff, and community. Note also that these are all local rules. There is no reference to the center or the head of the flock. Note also that the leading bird can change course for whatever reason, maybe a gust of wind, and the flock still hangs together. From these very simple rules complex patterns of great beauty can emerge. Surface complexity can arise from deep simplicity.

This now explains why the workshop we conducted for the network in 2006 was called "Deep Simplicity." Our aim was to foster discussion about what were the minimal, deeply simple rules that would allow us all to fly independently, in a self-organized manner, and still enjoy the benefits of flocking: survival and "thrival." By survival, we mean that birds flock for safety; the network offers resilience. By thrival, we mean that birds share work at the head of the peloton; the network shares leadership. Both help the community (or flock).

## Try This Thought Experiment

How about a walk in the park? We are about to participate in a thought experiment we call the BOIDS exercise.

Imagine, if you will, you are with our group at some outdoor location. We've done this exercise for real at an English manor house, a Bangkok hotel, an Italian *agriturismo*, and Balmoral Beach in Sydney (of course).

Imagine Ric (our complex systems expert) standing to one side, and saying, "I'm curious about how groups behave. Would you be good enough to follow the instructions I am going to give?" I will imagine you give guarded assent.

He continues, "Please select two other members of the group but don't disclose to them who they are. When you have done that, position yourself so you are equidistant from each."

You choose Max and Mary. You try to stand equidistant from each of them. In doing so, you realize this does not necessarily mean between them, or even close to them, but just equidistant. Just when you think you've nailed it, Mary moves. So you move, too, to preserve the equidistant rule. But as she settles Max moves, presumably because one of his chosen pair has moved, probably as a consequence of some other movement. As you contemplate this absurdity, you resign yourself to the fact this could take hours.

But to your surprise, it takes only a couple of minutes. Ric continues, "Now I'm going to ask you to do a group task. Who would be willing to volunteer as leader for this?" Ross volunteers.

"Thanks, Ross. Here's the task. I'd like you to lead the group to the other side of the garden, next to that oak tree. Over there, you must all be in an equidistant relationship relative to your chosen pair."

Ross suspects there is a trick to this, but he says, "Well, I think the easiest way to do this is if we all move as one." There's a murmur of approval. Alice seems to want to say something but decides better of it.

"Follow me," says Ross. "Let's all turn to face the tree. Now let's all take 10 steps forward and then stop." He counts off the steps without incident. However, it is apparent that this trajectory will bring Roland (who is out on the right flank) into contact with the children's playground equipment. Ross proves adaptable and changes direction for a while. "Let's all take 10 steps to the left." And so on, until Elizabeth, who is watching Ross and her two partners closely, steps in a hole where a sprinkler is hidden. Not only does she get wet, she hurts her ankle. Ross is nonplussed. He is tempted to suggest she sit out but then realizes the whole structure can unravel if she does. Bravely, she says, "Don't worry. I'll be OK." Ross continues, but more cautiously. You can sense the pressure he feels. He takes more time to scan the surroundings before giving the next instructions. Then, after 7 or 8 minutes, it's all over.

Ric invites the group to rest. "Any comments on what just happened?"

Alice says she has a question. "Is the point of the exercise so we are in the equidistant arrangement on the other side of the park?"

Ric says, "Yes."

"So we don't *have* to stay in that relationship all the way?" "No," says Ric.

"Can I try something?" Alice follows up. "Sure," says Ric.

"OK, everyone stand up. I'll see you over there [she points to another tree] where we can reassemble according to the equidistant rule." And she strides off on her own. Others hesitate then follow. Some walk around obstacles; all avoid water sprinklers; some pause at a water fountain for a drink; several pair up and chat; all choose their own pace.

Over by the tree the group reforms quickly, not in exactly the same pattern as might be seen by an outside observer, but all conforming to the equidistant rule of which there are limitless variations. People applaud

Alice's ingenuity. Ross looks a trifle embarrassed at first and then thought-ful. He's already asking himself what this means.

Ric continues his debrief. He reassures Ross that most times the "let's all stay in formation" option is adopted.

"Indeed, what did you expect?" he asks the group. The response is clear: Ross met their expectations of a leader. He was decisive: taking control, instilling confidence (at least at first), and relieving others of the need to devise a strategy. In short, he put himself out there as leader.

"Did Alice's approach also work?" "Yes."

"Is this also leadership?" Hesitation.

"Well, did it help the group get the task done?" "Yes."

"Efficiently?" "Yes."

"Safely?" Elizabeth, still rubbing her ankle, says, "Yes!"

"Was it easier, walking at your own pace, maybe chatting to a friend?" "Yes."

"I noticed people made their own decisions about how to avoid trees, rocks, and so on. Could we agree you shared in the decision making?" "Yes," again.

"So what was necessary for completion of the task?" There is general agreement the essentials were an understanding of the basics: the overall purpose, the equidistant rule, taking responsibility for one's self, and trust that others would cooperate.

"Who exercised control the first time?"

"Ross."

"And the second time?" Someone said Alice, but then someone else said, "All of us." General nodding greeted this remark.

Soon after, the group returns inside to a conference room. Ric says, "So let's see how we might use this idea. We came here today to focus on this question: *How can we improve our marketing performance?* Marketing is a big field. Some of you have experience in one form or another; some of you have questions about different aspects. Would you like to organize yourselves into discussion groups that suit your interest?"

One voice volunteers, "I want to know how to use social media."

Another says, "I'll join you in that."

Yet another says, "I went to a conference last week on digital market-ing. Can I join you?" A group starts to form and to negotiate the focus.

David says, "I'd like to talk to Roger about direct mail. He's the expert." Roger agrees to join David, and another cluster starts to form. And so on. Four groups emerge.

Ric says, "Take 30 minutes and then report back to the larger group, OK? Oh, and if you're not contributing to the discussion, or learning from it, then please feel free to move on. In fact, I encourage that." A half-hour later, four summaries are presented.

In Thailand, this exercise was so well received that we abandoned our agenda for the network conference starting the next day and adopted a similar approach (Open Space) for all of it, not just half as planned. It was a breakthrough; TOYFNET meeting attendance has gone up since.

Thanks for joining in. Did you enjoy it? Did it stimulate your thinking about leadership?

BOIDS, and birds flocking, are good, new metaphors for networked organizations and for us, a lot more helpful than military metaphors.

## Takeaways From Chapter 6

- The stereotypes of leadership are confining.
- The language of leadership perpetuates out-of-date metaphors.
- It takes time to unlearn these old metaphors: even experts appear confused.
- New metaphors yield insights: quantum physics, biology, computing, network science.
- The leader as host works well for networked organizations.
- The hub hosts conversations, ambitions, and meaning.
- The BOIDS model is one way of thinking about shared leadership and an organization's deep simplicity.
- A flock or community can help members, avian or human, to survive and thrive.

# CHAPTER 7

# Convening Coalitions

## An Unfinished Symphony

In chapter 2, we introduced a road map. It outlined three stages that we also referred to as phases, and we invoked the metaphor of phase change—solid to liquid to gas. If our metaphor had instead been a symphony, we have come to the third, and unfinished, movement. It may prove to be the most harmonious of them all.

It seems fair to ask, why go beyond crafting connections *and* community? Why not be satisfied with that? We would have said the same if we hadn't stumbled into phase 3 and started enjoying the benefits. Having done so, we can now say it transformed our business yet again. If in phase 1 we were doing well, and in phase 2, we were getting better, then in phase 3 we learned how to get better at getting better.

In this chapter, I will answer the following questions:

- What do we mean by a coalition and by network-to-network networking (N2N)?
- How did this occur?
- Why introduce our affiliates to other networks?
- What is N2Netiquette?
- How has N2N turbocharged our business?
- What is unfinished?
- What are the advantages of convening a coalition?

## What Do We Mean by a Coalition of Networks and by N2N?

Forming a coalition is about moving from a connected network, as shown in Figure 7.1, to a coalition of networks, as shown in Figure 7.2.

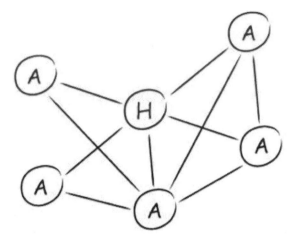

*Figure 7.1.  A phase 2 network or a community of connections.*

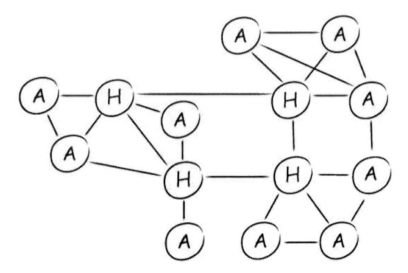

*Figure 7.2.  A phase 3 network or a coalition of communities.*

This might also be called a collection of hubs. But it's more than just hubs. Hubs, by definition, don't exist without affiliates, so affiliates inevitably become part of this. This is our N2N networking group. It is a coalition of people with like interests: people building networks, learning how to do it, and sharing insights with each other. And it has turbocharged our businesses. Two of the networks involved (one of them ours) have been introduced to their biggest affiliates via N2N. Suffice to say, this group now has a life of its own and we are unsure of where it will all end.

## How Did This Occur?

It's only in recent times we have dignified this activity with the N2N tag. It started more modestly as simple acts of helping mates—"mates" being an Australian term for good friends. In 1992, Michael Morgan of Herrmann Asia invited me to a workshop in the Blue Mountains just out of Sydney. Possibly, he was short of numbers. If so, there is a time-honored tradition of using family and mates to fill workshops as necessary.

During this event, I sat next to Magdalene Sik from Singapore. When we moved to Singapore in 1993, it was only natural to connect with her. Magdalene became an affiliate of ours and, 20 years later, has developed the world's largest client for our products. I was grateful to Michael for the introduction of course but at the time didn't see the significance of this as a new phase. To borrow a phrase from our industry, I was unconsciously competent: I was doing the right thing but unable to generalize about it.

Because Michael was also building an Asian business, he regularly used our apartment-cum-office in Singapore as his hotel. Our collaboration flourished. He became a regular guest at our network meetings, often contributing as a facilitator. In return, I attended some of Michael's network meetings. Last year, I ran one for him. Michael and I meet every 2 months for lunch at Balmoral and sail once or twice a year on his yacht.

In 1998, when I moved to Europe, Michael introduced me to his counterpart in Germany, Roland Spinola. Roland became our Mr. Germany. He and his wife have become close friends. Roland introduced me to the world of alternative currencies and to Bernard Lietaer, whose work on sustainable systems and resilience is referenced in chapter 3.

In 2001, Michael and I decided to run a combined network meeting, but not just any meeting. We both invited our worldwide partners and affiliates to join us in a large Tuscan villa. When we committed to the rent of US$35,000, we shuddered at the financial risk. In the end, we filled it to overflowing. We called the meeting "Network Conversazione."

It was exciting. We ran parallel and joint sessions. Most of us had a partner with us and, in one case, a whole family. Another brought his wife for their 20th wedding anniversary. We combined work and pleasure. Everyone was invited to contribute from their hobbies and passions. The results included an a cappella choir, a watercolor group, photography lessons, a tour of the nearby da Vinci museum, Italian language lessons, and much more—all led by members of our networks. It was a celebration of strengths, independence, community, and all things Italian. The lines between work and nonwork were wonderfully blurred—an idea captured in Semler's book title *The Seven-Day Weekend*[1]—which, after all, is why many of us are corporate refugees.

Today, this event lives on in two forms: The first is an international N2N meeting held every couple of years, over several days, and also in Italy (so far). The second is N2N Sydney, which meets every few months for a 4-hour meeting and lunch. In both cases, we share similar interests. We are all building international networks based on training products. Rarely do we compete. If we do, it is more likely for a share of the client's training budget than head on. But there are many more things that unite us: learning about markets, swapping contracting insights, learning how to run worthwhile network meetings, and asking for help to find affiliates in a specific country, to mention a few.

## Why Introduce Our Affiliates to Each Other?

When Michael attended *our* network meetings, he met potential affiliates for *his* network, and vice versa. This worked for everyone. Recall the affiliates had asked me from the beginning to introduce them to additional products. And when they had them, I no longer felt as concerned that their ability to feed their families depended on only the product we supplied (an early instinct about resilience). At one point, 70% of Michael's network and ours overlapped.

But it still strikes some as odd that we should collaborate in this way. Their argument might run like this: Surely, if one of your affiliates takes on someone else's products, this will only distract them from selling yours.

This sounds plausible, especially if one assumes a zero sum world. But we find this isn't the case. We find that the collaboration works for all. Consider the following observations:

1. The affiliate usually wants a range of products to offer to their clients. They will find other products with our help or without it. They know we often know what's happening in the broader industry. Were we to withhold useful information, it would send several messages, such as we don't care about your overall success, only our own, or we doubt you are capable of expanding to cope with extra work. Neither of these messages is good for our relationship. They only diminish the trust on which, ultimately, our relationship is based.

2. It also says we ignore what they clearly asked us for. At our very first Think on Your Feet Network (TOYFNET) meeting, when we asked what we could do for them, they were very clear: "Help us find other products." If you ask, you must listen. If you then ignore what they say, you can forget about asking again.

3. It aligns us with their futures. Our status changes subtly but significantly from being suppliers to partners. In turn, they revise their default assumption of not trusting us. And they reciprocate; they care about *our* future, too. The relationship becomes increasingly valuable to both parties. Social capital accumulates. It brings the economies of trust into the business relationship.

4. The relationship becomes more open. They tend not to withhold information; nor do we. We sometimes show our financial results at network meetings: They know we have nothing to hide. Increasingly, they share their information.

5. N2N gives us extra security. Imagine for a moment we suspect an affiliate of ripping us off in some way. What could I do? I'd call others in our N2N network doing business with the same affiliate and ask if they had any reason to share my concerns. You can imagine the potential value in this—if we ever had to use it.

6. We also find better candidates. Laurent Choppe of the N.E.W.S. Coaching network said to me, "Since we have been in the N2N relationship we have found more affiliate candidates, more quickly, and in more countries than ever before. But most importantly, they are of a higher caliber."

7. We help each other design better businesses. At an N2N meeting, network builders swap ideas, share concerns, and build relationships for the future. Because networked organizations are not yet well understood, we turn to each other to learn. We have practical

questions, like how to attract affiliates to network meetings. One of our members, Adina Luca, has interviewed many of us, researched the similarities and differences in our models, and presented her findings to spark an N2N discussion. (See resource 3.)

Having thought about it long and hard and having experienced the benefits, introducing affiliates to other hubs is very worthwhile. One key is to do it thoughtfully, observing what we call N2Netiquette.

## What is N2Netiquette?

In personal life, you would take care about who to introduce to whom and how you did it. The same applies in introducing hubs and affiliates. Imagine, if you will, that you introduce an affiliate of yours to another hub who treats that person less than well, commits an unrealized cultural faux pas, or generally does not make you, the introducer, look good. This is a tricky situation. You may need to repair things with the affiliate or give polite but corrective feedback to the fellow hub.

The playbook for these situations is yet to be written, but I imagine most of the following will feature when it has been:

- Remember Axelrod and his advice: Be generous to start, reciprocate when generosity is returned, and defect (or, better, have a chat) when it's not.
- Don't waste people's time. In a fictitious example, let's imagine Brazil is the next hot market. Your affiliate there is a gem. He is working extremely long hours just to cope with his growth. He wants new ideas, but he has precious little time to evaluate them—especially in his second language. In this case, have a chat with him first to discover his priorities—if indeed you want to serve him in this way. Then act with his interests coming first.
- When offering an introduction, suggest how the affiliate might be treated.
- When offered one, ask about how the affiliate ought to be treated.
- When you receive a connection, treat it like a gem. Guard it, protect the interests of your introducer, and don't leave it lying

around for others to borrow. It is not yours to pass on until you have earned that right.

- Don't hand an affiliate list to others unless you have permission to do so.
- Choose to collaborate only with hubs who share similar values about affiliates.
- Find ways for people to encounter each other; let them decide who they want to talk to. N2N meetings allow this to happen.
- Make it clear you don't want to be copied on all their e-mails. Also make it clear to the receiver of your gift (of an introduction) it would be nice if they let you know what happened.
- Consider showing gratitude in some significant way—either symbolically or otherwise.
- If it's otherwise, like money or similar, and it was arranged beforehand, then declare this to your affiliate in advance.
- Avoid conflicts of interest.

All of this is common sense. But sometimes we are in too much of a hurry to remember; sometimes a hub can get red mist, too.

## How Has N2N Turbocharged Our Business?

I might have headed this section as *How to Find a Trustworthy Partner in China*. This would reflect the concern some have for protecting their intellectual property (IP) interests. Let me be clear: I have spent years of my life in the company of Chinese people. They are not untrustworthy. However, it is fair to say that IP rights are not regarded the same in all countries. As Adina, an expert on cross-cultural differences, tells me, there is for many a belief that knowledge is a community asset and that it cannot be owned by individuals or companies. And in this context, what Westerners call lack of trust is simply a different philosophy regarding ownership. Her explanation gives an enlightened view of trust. But if the assumptions behind your business model require IP to be protected (and ours do), your task in a different culture is to find someone sympathetic to your views.

So in a country where authentic copies of Windows are hard to find, how do we find this person or persons? This is a search for information, not unlike looking for a new job. So we follow Mark Granovetter's advice and ask our weak (as well as our strong) networks.[2] In this case, the best information is likely to come from others setting up international networks in the training business—that is, N2N. And so it has turned out. It took us years to find the right partner in China, but it was worth the wait.

Then Brian Emmanuel introduced us to Jeremy, whom you've already met. Brian is also based in Sydney, and we meet two or three times a year for coffee or lunch (at Balmoral). When recommending Jeremy, Brian's exact words were "you can trust him." This has turned out to be true. I had occasion to remind Jeremy of this over dinner in Shanghai recently. We were talking about who and when to trust in business. Jeremy said that a common assumption about people's motives is that self-interest is the best guide. This might be so. However, I suddenly felt the need to share my conviction that it's worth taking the trouble to find those you can trust. So I said with feeling, "Jeremy, I believe it *is* possible to trust some people. I trust you. You were recommended as trustworthy. Until I find out otherwise, I hold to that. Actually, I have little option. You could rip me off any time you like. But I don't believe you would." There was a short silence while we both digested what I'd said. It was a clarifying moment in our relationship. Later, I saw it in the context of a role we spoke about in the last chapter—the custodian of meaning.

When I got back to Sydney, I reflected on that exchange and realized how much we both owe to Brian. I called Jeremy to suggest we celebrate Brian's introduction. He agreed. A few weeks later, Brian and his wife were guests of honor at a dinner in Sydney. We presented him with an original scroll commissioned by Jeremy in Shanghai. It hangs 2 meters long and bears this inscription in beautifully hand-painted Chinese calligraphy:

Brian:
>    You gave us the gift of an introduction.
>    You said we could trust each other.
>    We did, and it has been better than we imagined.
>    We are very grateful.

Warmly,
Jeremy and Ken

If I now reveal that Jeremy is our largest affiliate, and we are his biggest supplier, the significance of that original introduction comes sharply into focus. And if you also recall I met Magdelene via Michael (i.e., via N2N before we thought to call it that), that she has developed our largest client in the world, and that these are just the most obvious of many benefits, it's easy to see why I say N2N, or convening a coalition, has turbocharged our businesses.

## What Is Unfinished?

I don't know what is unfinished, but I can imagine a few possibilities, including expanding N2N, N2N business services, and N2N *inside* normal organizations:

1. *Expanding N2N.* I can see the potential to embrace our wider eco-system of clients, suppliers, academia, and industry bodies as well (see Figure 7.3).

    Here's a topical example that helped two hubs, their affiliates, and a client lift productivity in a downturn.

    Early 2010 was tough. The global financial crisis was biting. In January, when I called Keith Dugdale, hub for the Smarter Selling network, he was at home watching cricket on television. (January is holiday time in Australia.) We joked that our affiliates might be watching a lot of cricket this year. Then we got serious. What could

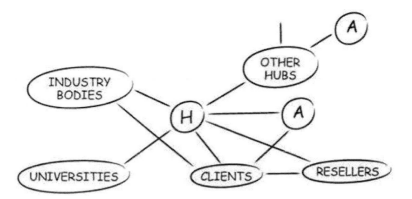

*Figure 7.3. An extended N2N network or coalition.*

we do about this waste of resources? It helped no one. Our clients were in a slow period, too. We speculated about possibilities.

The result was a free series of workshops offered to our affiliates. Keith ran his workshop for our affiliates, and vice versa. We found a client willing to give us a conference room in exchange for some free seats. A plus for us was our networks might be able to recognize opportunities for each other in future. It worked. Both teams got a skills upgrade. A client relationship was cemented. Two more affiliates joined us (despite not having this as an objective). And less cricket was watched for a few days.

2. *N2N business services.* These services could include ad hoc consulting, long-term mentoring, transaction services, shared facilities, investor introductions, and more. They could be offered to those within one's own N2N group or to those outside it.

Offering advice to those *inside* your own N2N group is expected, and receiving it might simply be a privilege of membership. On the other hand, perhaps a new hub wants to receive more than the normal exchange. So we have the possibility to offer these services as either freeware (trusting that what goes around comes around, or simply that we enjoy the giving, or both) or as "feeware." How to do this is an unfinished discussion.

3. *Inside a nonnetworked organization.* There are a growing number of executives who agree with Rob Cross and Andrew Parker that social networks are the way work *really* gets done in modern, knowledge work enterprises.[3] Some want to run normal company structures as networks. Take as an example the results-only work environment (ROWE) type of organization. Daniel Pink gives the example of Meddius, a hospital IT specialist, which changed from everyone working similar hours, in the same office, to working when and where they liked, just as long as the work got done.[4] After a period of adjustment, staff productivity rose and stress declined.

These are now network-like organizations, but with employees. Helping them to adapt, to build internal communities, and to form their own N2N groups is imaginable, even likely.

## What Are the Advantages of Convening a Coalition?

The advantages of convening a coalition include the following:

- Faster recruitment of affiliates
- Pretested affiliates
- Access to more countries
- Faster business growth
- Lower costs
- Avoidance of traps
- Potential for group influence on shared affiliates
- Borrowing of other hubs for events, making us all more leader-full
- Benefits for our affiliates, and therefore our relationships
- Introductions to trusted service providers, such as lawyers, hotels, translators, printers, shipping agents, government export-import services and subsidies, and more
- Community in the form of encouragement, solace, fun, support, and an opportunity to contribute

In short, it's a way to get better at getting better.

## Takeaways From Chapter 7

- The phase change can be seen in Figure 7.4.
- The potential is to embrace our wider ecology of clients, suppliers, academia, and industry bodies (see Figure 7.5).
- There is a need for N2Netiquette.
- N2N offers a way to turbocharge the business.
- It's unfinished business.

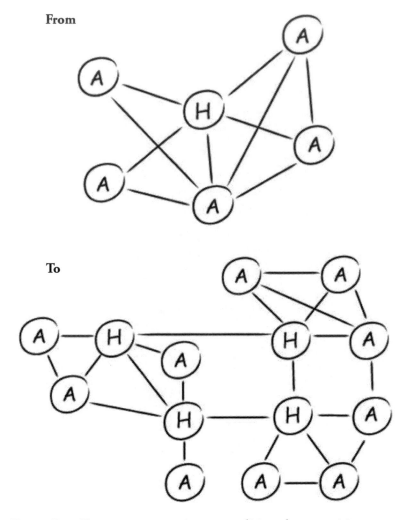

Figure 7.4. *From one community to a coalition of communities.*

To

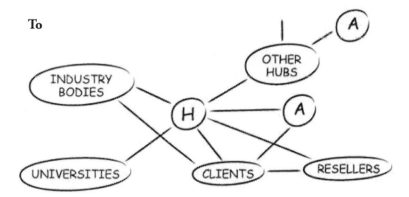

*Figure 7.5. From an N2N network to an extended N2N network.*

# CHAPTER 8

# Suffocating a Network

After so much effort invested in building networks, why now choose to suffocate one? Think of the locksmith teaching a burglar to rob premises he has just secured. If this test works, it shows the locksmith understands his design well. Likewise, starting with the essentials of good networks as we have laid them out and then predicting successfully how to unlock (or suffocate) one is some kind of validation for our theories about networks. Fortunately, we have no need to cripple a real network. That has already been done for us. We are therefore able to inspect the remains to see if it has been done in the way we would have predicted.

This chapter is therefore both tongue-in-cheek and tragic. It's tongue-in-cheek because it's the last thing we would advocate, plus it contains some mild fiction. It's tragic because it happened. The good news is it usually happens because of a category error made by hubs who think of networks as a variant of normal, hierarchical organizations. This is a misunderstanding we hope this book has by now dispelled. So let's suffocate a network—in our imaginations.

We shall ask the following questions:

- How could you do it in principle?
- How would this work in practice?
- How are we doing in our case study?
- What actually happened?
- What does this tell us?

## How Could You Do It in Principle?

We've proposed the foundations of a successful networked organization as the following:

- Independence
- Community
- Shared stuff

Under shared stuff, we've highlighted the importance of trust and a collaborative mind-set. And we've noted Daniel Pink's take on this that high motivation for our kind of people arises from autonomy, mastery, and purpose.[1]

Therefore if we take these away, do we suffocate a network? Are David Limerick and Bert Cunnington right that these things are the organizational glue?[2] If so, removing one or more should be a good starting point in our macabre experiment: remove the glue and the network should come unstuck. With these hypotheses to guide us, how do we actually do it? Do you have any ideas?

## How Would You Do It in Practice?

What follows is a case study. It is a figment of my imagination. The company Guru Management, the Guru, Helen, and Ivan are all fictional. But the detail is true. It all happened but not all in the same network and not at the same time.

Once upon a time there was a European guru with his business called Guru Management. The Guru made a name for himself via workshops, books, television appearances, charisma, and tireless travel. From early on others wanted to join in spreading his word. So the Guru started accrediting them to use his technology. In truth, the technology predated the Guru, but his followers were willing to acknowledge his role in packaging and popularizing it and cough up royalties for the rights to use it.

Things went well. The Guru's calendar became more crowded; more affiliates joined; more help was needed. He recruited Helen as network manager. She had a very strong administrative background in corporate life. He also allocated her some shares in the business. She embraced the opportunity to clean things up and get things under control.

As a start, she commissioned a strategy review and did serious brainstorming with some consultants. Three critical success factors emerged: building the brand, growth, and revenue enhancement. The core idea, however, was the role of the brand. To operationalize this (as one consultant put it), Helen persuaded the Guru as follows:

- All affiliates would brand their businesses as Guru Management, too. That is, business cards, letterheads, websites, and the like were to be branded Guru Management. Then they would add something like "Represented by Catherine Damon," "Nordic Management," or similar.
- Billing should be centralized to ensure consistency, to underscore the branding strategy, and to support revenue enhancement.
- Any sales involving more than one country would be handled by Guru Management headquarters.
- The affiliate contract should be amended to reflect these initiatives.

The Guru approved, happy to have someone else looking after these things while he focused on his enthusiastic audiences. If you think about it, he really had little choice. Having hired Helen and allocated her some shares, it would have been extremely difficult to disagree (and part with her) before she had even had a chance to fix things. And the carefully assembled arguments of high-priced consultants made everything seem so reasonable.

At short notice, a network meeting was called in Florence (always an attraction) to introduce the changes. The Guru kicked it off in rousing style. Helen followed with highlights of the new strategy, assured everyone they would like the details, and then introduced the agenda. The first item was the signing of new contracts. She didn't want to unveil the really exciting details to any who were not committed.

This was a dramatic note to start on, to be sure, but the Guru had set the scene for success with his rallying cry. Of course, it wasn't compulsory to sign the contract. And if people preferred not to, they were welcome to leave as friends. They could continue to sell Guru Management products for 1 more year. Given all of this—the sense of anticipation, plus the investment they'd already made in Guru Management to date, plus the expense of flying to Florence (which was yet to be explored), and having very little time to mull things over (let alone discuss them among themselves)—they signed. It was difficult not to, despite their misgivings.

However, some had not been able to get to the meeting because of the short notice given and prior commitments. It took only until morning coffee for them to find out what was happening via calls from concerned colleagues present. Away from the hothouse of the conference, they pondered on what this all meant.

## How Are We Doing in Our Case Study?

How are the Guru and Helen doing so far in our little fiction? Remember, we've assigned them the role of suffocating the network. Let's review our list. Think about whether they have done any of the following:

- Reduced or improved independence or autonomy
- Ignored or embraced collaborative strategies
- Damaged or supported shared values
- Diminished or developed the affiliates' sense of mastery
- Overlooked or highlighted shared purpose
- Lost or enhanced trust

I think the answers are pretty clear. They've reduced, ignored, damaged, diminished, overlooked, and lost.

So what has gone wrong? Do we imagine the Guru and Helen want to damage their network? Do they think that will happen? I believe no. So why are they taking these risks? And what is wrong, I ask you, with their aims to build the brand, to grow, and to enhance revenue? These kinds of things come straight from the Management 101 playbook.

And that's the problem. The Management 101 playbook assumes a traditional company, either privately or publicly owned. And a traditional company has employees, not affiliates. This means that, first, the owners have the right to set the agenda, and second, while they might be clumsy in gaining support, there are few if any conflicts with employee interests in what is proposed. A healthy company means a better company to work for, does it not? Simply put, these strategies, if announced to employees, could sound eminently sensible.

But affiliates are not employees. (See chapter 3.) They have different contracts, both legal and emotional. It's not hard to see why affiliates might be threatened by Helen's announcements. And the ultimatum to change or else raised the question of how much reliance they should place on their futures with Guru Management.

## What Actually Happened?

Ivan, not at the meeting, shared his thoughts with me:

- He supported a strong brand. He knew this would help sell the Guru's books and videos and even help his own business. On the other hand, it would make it difficult for Ivan to represent the other products he carried, which had nothing to do with Guru Management. He imagined this was an oversight. (Could it be they didn't know?)
- But Ivan had a brand, too. He'd carefully built it over 7 years and wasn't inclined to abandon this investment. In fact, he thought hiding his brand to give Guru Management preeminence was a bad idea.
- As for the billing, he had no problem with that. He'd actually end up with the same amount of money, so that seemed OK. It just meant Guru Management would take out their royalty first and then pay him for selling or delivering. Up until now it had been the other way around.
- Unfortunately, Helen had positioned this as a revenue enhancement program, which made Ivan curious. Whose revenue was she enhancing? He assumed it was the Guru's. So why? Was Helen's pay package partly revenue based? Could there be other reasons? He consulted his accountant. He was told that, in some countries, businesses could be sold for multiples of revenue. If this was motivating the Guru, he could get a higher price for his business if he later sold it. Ivan saw immediately this made *his* business less valuable if the same formula applied because he would record less revenue even though his profit might not change. This now disturbed him. What at first had

seemed to be an administrative device of little consequence
could actually have a sting in the tail: a loss of value for Ivan.

- The loss of transnational sales also bothered him. He was in a
Baltic country. He had built good relations with his neighbor-
ing affiliates. They understood each other and in several cases
spoke each others' languages. He'd already done one big deal
with the Baltic headquarters of a Big Four accounting house
and happily subcontracted delivery to his colleagues around
the region. They had been optimistic about more such collaborations. Had these opportunities disappeared?

- The way the meeting had been conducted bothered him, too.
Previously, the Guru had encouraged a collegial atmosphere.
This seemed to have evaporated. In fairness, one affiliate did
say that Helen showed strong leadership.

- Ivan's final comment was revealing: "It's easier to dismiss affiliates than employees," he said. "There are rules protecting the
latter in many European countries."

He and some others, therefore, declined to accept the changes. After
many years' association, and significant investment, they decided to drop
Guru Management products, with great regret.

Ivan decided to do some research on the origins of Guru Management
and, thanks to the wonders of the web, he found an obscure product that
looked similar. To his surprise, he discovered this version was available
from the Guru's original mentor. He contacted the mentor and found
he could get an exclusive license, not only for his country, but for the
entire Baltic region. Best of all, he could retain full control of his brand
and revenue. To top it all off, the royalties were lower. He called his Baltic
neighbors, some of whom joined him immediately. A couple of these had
suspected a weakness in the Guru's intellectual property protection all
along but out of respect for him had not bothered to look for, let alone
exploit, any supposed loopholes. For them, the relationship mattered.
Now, however, it seemed it did not matter so much to the Guru, so they
defected, and Guru Management could take no action. Ivan was now a
hub, and he set about building his own network.

# What Does This Tell Us?

First, it's important to understand the deep simplicity of an organization or what makes it tick. Otherwise, it is easy to stop its functioning. A good analogy might be putting regular gasoline into the tank of a diesel car. A simple misunderstanding brings things to a halt.

Second, sometimes it's the process, rather than the content, that surfaces values. Take, for example, the billing question: Should it be centralized or not? One of the longest standing networks in the Asia-Pacific has always billed centrally. The reason was to improve marketing success while maintaining fair shares of the rewards. The idea was that all parties to a sale received fixed proportions of the revenue. The simple formula was one-third to the seller, one-third to the deliverer (who might also be the seller), and one-third to the hub. Meanwhile, pricing was allowed to flex as required by local markets. Facilitators in Thailand are not as expensive as those in Japan. Therefore Thai clients expect to pay less for a workshop than the Japanese. This scheme allowed for pricing to be determined by the local markets and affiliates. This actually increased their perceived autonomy and improved their chances of sales. The cost, if any, of centralized billing was seen as a small inconvenience to pay for more sales. And when put like this, the sharing model came across as a revenue enhancement program *for all*. In the case of Guru Management, though, the centralization idea, announced in a climate of suspicion, was not seen as constructive.

Third, the real issue here was probably the issue of trust. A reservoir of trust, accumulated over time, helps a great deal in times of change. In the Guru's case, trust was diminished by the way things were done.

Fourth, language matters. Employers can say to employees, "We have reviewed X and decided Y." And they can send e-mails along these lines:

Please find attached the output of the Grow Guru Management task force. At our meeting next week we will unveil our new plans . . . It's clear these initiatives are necessary for us to grow the world market . . . to be global but act local . . . We will need to [take some action] . . . It will become too difficult to coordinate otherwise . . . [etc.].

These announcements would be considered unremarkable by employees, even if full of corporate-speak. But saying or sending the same to affiliates might provoke different reactions. (See resource 5.)

Finally, engagement matters. Engagement has become a popular way to talk about and measure the willingness of employees to invest energy, ideas, and time in their work. Research by Gallup and others tells us high engagement companies have significantly higher earnings growth.[3] What is sometimes overlooked is that with independent affiliates, engagement comes for free. Affiliates have, to a large extent, tailored their work-life to be engaging, because they have choices. And the hub enjoys the fruits of this engagement bonus as part of the networked design. But if a hub ignores affiliate needs, engagement dissipates—slowly at first and then more rapidly. In Ivan's case, it became total, *and* it spread through the network, destroying the hub's reputation and the community with it.

In summary, ways for hubs to suffocate networks include the following:

- Confusing the manager-employee and hub-affiliate models
- Adding corporate-like controls, which are often unnecessary for affiliates, who feel a loss of autonomy
- Creating silos by interposing the hub between affiliates in collaborations. This might seem sensible (a need to know what's going on), until you realize this can reduce connectedness, community, innovation, and leadership
- Submerging identity, such as was the case with the branding issue, which feels, again, like a loss of autonomy
- Making declarations during meetings, which is not as effective as hosting conversations

## Takeaways From Chapter 8

- Remember the essential differences between the manager-employee and hub-affiliate models (see Figure 8.1).
- Try to *increase* affiliate independence, community, *and* the sense of shared stuff.
- Recognize these as the path to achieving one's *own* goals.
- Remember that networks are quick to spread good and bad news, and you have less control over this than with employees.
- If you also have employees, remember the differences.

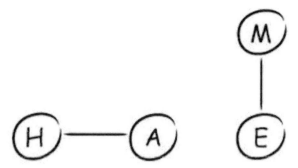

*Figure 8.1. The hub-affiliate and manager-employee relationships contrasted.*

- Recall that internal networks are how work *really* gets done[4] anyway and act just as carefully. Employees can disengage, too, and you may have no way of knowing.
- Remind yourself of the pluses independent affiliates bring: resilience, quality, self-management, higher productivity, innovation, reach, lower costs, and shared leadership.
- Ask yourself whether it makes sense to risk suffocating an organism that provides these advantages.

In the next chapter, let's examine some examples of what can happen when things are done well.

# CHAPTER 9

# Organizations, Networks, Communities, and Hybrids

We started our journey with three provocations based on the Internet, Visa, and the Think on Your Feet Network (TOYFNET). Other writers have examined other network-like organizations, including Mozilla, Linux, and Wikipedia. In this chapter, I offer a further selection that some might consider quirky, from both old and new, from both high-tech and low-tech, and from both the Northern and Southern Hemispheres. Each offers insights and each passes our test: They all demonstrate independence, community, and shared stuff, and they each offer ideas for today's organization architects.

Let's start with something old *and* low-tech. Let's look at a network of workers who have only the basics of education.

## India and the *Dabbawalas* of Mumbai

Networking and lunch often go together. But Mumbai's famous *dabbawalas* bring them together in an entirely new way. Their network delivers home-prepared lunches to the desks of office workers. *Dabba* means "lunch box or tin"; *wala* means "a person who carries."

Taking your lunch to work on Mumbai's crowded commuter trains is difficult. However, many workers prefer to eat home-cooked food for reasons of dietary choice, economy, or hygiene. The dabbawalas solve this problem by delivering home-prepared meals.

Each day, the meal is packed in its dabba to be ready for collection by 9:00 a.m. A dabbawala collects around 40 boxes and takes them, usually by bike, to the local railway station. Each box carries a unique destination code that is understood by all the dabbawalas. Using the codes, the dabbas are sorted into destination groups, ready for loading onto trains around 10:00 a.m. The dabbawalas accompany the lunch boxes. Each alights at a station in Mumbai with around 40 boxes. This group of 40 boxes is not the dabbawala's original 40, which were from his clients. These boxes are for a specific delivery area. They are whisked to workers' desks, arriving within a few minutes of 12:30 p.m. each day. This takes considerable skill and effort. Then the dabbawalas, in groups, take a short break to eat their own lunch, which they have also carried. Around 1:30 p.m. they collect the empty containers, reverse the morning process, and return the containers by 6:00 p.m., ready for cleaning and reuse the next day.

A few things should be noted:

- There is no home address on the box, only the delivery address.
- There are no receipts or other documentation; all is done on trust and reputation.
- They have an obsession for punctuality and reliability.
- All of this costs less than a lunch bought in Mumbai.
- The dabbawalas are independent entrepreneurs who work in small groups.
- Each group is assisted by a senior dabbawala who acts as a local hub. He (there are few women dabbawalas) distributes the monies received, hosts weekly meetings, and settles the rare disputes.
- Their reliability level (one mistake in every 8 million deliveries, or 16 million counting the returns) is equivalent to the Six Sigma standard considered demanding in factories using modern equipment.
- The walas act alone to find clients but collaborate in delivery.
- The organization is very flat, given its 200,000 clients and 5,000 dabbawalas. It has only three levels—the dabbawalas, their seniors, and the Tiffinmen's Association (*tiffin* also means "lunch tin"), which oversees standards across all of Mumbai.
- Notably, all in the Tiffinmen's Association, at all levels, deliver lunches.
- Funding is via a small contribution from each man.
- Any surplus goes to a charitable trust that feeds the poor.

- They all come from one region and caste, so community is preloaded.
- The dabbawalas have been operating for 120 years.
- They are now experimenting with text messaging and web-based booking of the service, but their history demonstrates high-tech tools are not a prerequisite for an effective network.

### Comments

- They show both independence and collaboration.
- They share a strong sense of purpose, camaraderie, and excellence.
- Their common stuff includes their backgrounds and the transmission protocol.
- The dabbawala system has been likened to the Internet. It operates just like packet switching, which perhaps could have been called dabba switching.
- They achieve spectacular levels of quality and precision.
- The pride evident in their status and work ethic shows the potential for people in networks to establish their own identity.

Let's now move from low-tech to high-tech and from old to new.

## Germany and the SAP Community Network

In 2006 I decided to learn firsthand why we had difficulty in the German market. We could do business with German heavyweight companies like Deutsche Bank, SAP, and Mercedes in Singapore, Hong Kong, or Melbourne, but not in Germany. So I traveled the length and breadth of Germany on their excellent trains to meet people at places like BMW, IBM, and *managerSeminare* magazine. My meeting with SAP was on the phone with a most helpful human resources executive. At the end of our discussion, I asked if there was anything I could offer in return. Well, it seems I had mentioned networks during our conversation. She picked up on that and asked some probing questions. I later sent her some articles that seemed relevant and thought little more about it.

In retrospect, I could have learned a lot about networks from them. At that time SAP was implementing its SAP Community Network. This network is clearly SAP sponsored in terms of resources. But it has attracted huge non-SAP support. As of late 2010, there were over two million members, with 25,000 joining each month. It hosts 200,000 assets (papers, solutions, presentations, etc.) and receives 6,000 forum posts daily.

Its purpose is to connect SAP users, inside and outside SAP, so that each can tap the combined expertise for quick answers. And they get their answers quickly—normally within 20 minutes of posting a question. That's a remarkable service. Users can suggest product enhancements, and the community can vote on these. One can see what a bonus this is for both SAP and its users. One can also see that SAP has no place to hide. It has irrevocably opened itself, including its development priorities, up to the world. SAP calls this a client-focused ecosystem.[1] As one book put it, "Markets are conversations."[2]

One bonus I discovered is the opportunity for career growth it offers. Participation showcases expertise. One insightful post led to more business for the contributor's company and a promotion for himself. It's hard to see how this cannot benefit all involved—even SAP's competitors, I imagine.

### Footnotes to the SAP Community Example

1. We have an interesting connection to this system. David is an SAP user working with a plastics manufacturer in Melbourne. He is an expert in plant maintenance software. For many years he declined invitations to speak at industry conferences because he felt his public speaking skills were poor. In 2008, he decided enough was enough and attended a Think on Your Feet workshop. He gained enough confidence to host a worldwide webinar for the SAP Community Network.

2. One outcome of my visit to Germany was an interview with *managerSeminare* magazine. The headline translated to "The German Training Market Is an Island," which is a good approximation of my words: "The German border is nonporous for training."

    This was part of my explanation as to why there are excellent examples of German workshops used widely *within* Germany but rarely *outside it*. The most obvious example is the ubiquitous moderation technique. Every seminar room comes preequipped with the materials required to run such a session. It's as common as the overhead projector. On the other hand, non-German intellectual property is rarely adopted with gusto. This is the experience of others in our network-to-network (N2N) network. One of the benefits of N2N is the chance to discover you are not alone.

3. More company-backed communities are emerging. One such community is ex-employees. My invitation to join the Greater IBM Network read, "As a member, you will get the latest local news, be able to participate in face-to-face events and discussion forums, gain business insights, get Lenovo discounts and learn about job opportunities here and abroad." IBM clearly believes ex-employees can be part of their supportive ecosystem.

## Spain, the Basque, and Mondragon

The Basque Country, an autonomous community within Spain, is home to a bold organizational initiative called the Mondragon Corporation Cooperative (MCC).

### The Principles Behind the MCC

Under the banner of "Humanity at Work," the 100 companies within MCC (or cooperatives as they call them) operate in the following areas:

- Finance (banking)
- Industry (cars and construction)
- Distribution (hypermarkets)
- Knowledge (IT and higher education)

The following are MCC's stated corporate values:

- Cooperation
- Participation
- Social responsibility
- Innovation

Distinguishing features include their use of democratic methods in the organizing structure and the distribution of the assets generated for the benefit of members and the community. The democratic structure is reflected in the boards at all levels within the 100 cooperatives in the group. A total of 1,000 employees participate at board level. That's very different from the traditional one-board model. MCC's structure is similar in several respects to the old Visa system. (See chapter 1.)

Another feature is how they preserve humanity at work. Cooperatives are restricted to a human scale of 500 people or fewer. Beyond that, they are required to split, like an amoeba, to a more manageable scale, which is like nature's common response to complexity.

MCC is recognized as a leader in worker cooperation. The mother ship MCC hosts all the companies. It is custodian of the values the group espouses and a catalyst for collaboration among members. For example, the bank provides financing on condition that standards like the 500-employee limit are observed. But cooperatives are free to leave the group, and some have. From its origins in the 1950s, MCC has become a sizable enterprise:

- It is the number 1 company in the Basque Country and number 7 in Spain.
- It has 85,000 employees.
- As noted, there are 100 cooperatives.
- It generates €15 billion in revenues.

The size, longevity, and success of MCC give credibility to its business model, which is based on independent units, acting within a community, and sharing strong values.

MCC has been promoted as a model by governance experts like Professor Shann Turnbull. He says that typical corporate governance is primitive; Enron and subsequent failures are evidence of this. He singles out unitary board structures as a particular problem: "Command and control hierarchies are so ubiquitous that their shortcomings are accepted as the natural order . . . Network governance . . . provides the foundation for institutions to become genuinely self-governing."[3] He cites the old Visa example as one spectacularly successful form of governance and MCC as another.

# Brazil, Sao Paulo, and Semco

*Maverick* by Ricardo Semler tells how he introduced dramatic change at his company (Semco) after a life-threatening scare.[4] Semler's book was written in 1994. I gave away copies to friends, several of whom thought I was mad. Today his ideas look more sensible by the day. He recently featured in the Massachusetts Institute of Technology Sloan School of Management Dean's Innovative Leader Series 20 years after first implementing his ideas, namely, give people autonomy, unite them around core ideals, and collaborate across the group.[5]

## The Spark

Semler inherited Semco from his father at age 21. He threw himself into the business, working crazy hours, traveling constantly, and living to work. On a trip to the United States, Semler collapsed during a factory tour. Doctors assured him there was nothing seriously wrong with him, but if he kept going like he was, he would soon be using their brand new cardiac ward. He got the message.

## The Change

He was determined to balance his work and personal life more carefully and to allow the same for employees. He discovered this was not at odds with business success. The more freedom he gave staff, the more productive, loyal, and innovative they became. And the better it was for Semco. In the 6 years from 1998 to 2004, revenues jumped from US$35 million to US$212 million and staff from several hundred to 3,000, and all this with the miniscule employee turnover rate of 2%. (The UK average is 15%.) There is a waiting list of Brazil's best and brightest for jobs at Semco.

## The New Era of Autonomy and Shared Leadership

Staff at Semco are encouraged to do the following:

- Set their own schedules
- Evaluate their bosses

- Suggest their own salaries
- Work from any location: office, home, or beach
- Decorate their own workspace
- Dress as they wish
- Find work they like

Plus, there are the following benefits:

- There are two spare seats for employees at board meetings.
- Hiring takes place from within first and then from outside candidates.
- Candidates are all interviewed at once by the workers.
- Strikes are OK and considered part of normal work time.
- Financial records are open to employees.

In a later book, *The Seven-Day Weekend,* Semler focuses on work-leisure balance.[6] He says that if one is trying to achieve a balance, there is probably something wrong, either with the work, or the leisure, or both. Why should the two be at odds? Why can't work be natural?

In chapter 1 of his book he asks the following questions:

1. Why can we answer e-mails on Sundays but we are not able to go to the movies on Mondays?
2. Why can't we take the kids to work if we are able to take work home?
3. Why do we think the opposite of work is leisure when in fact it is idleness?

These are, when you think about it, questions about autonomy.

Semco's low turnover rate offers an interesting way to see how high engagement contributes to the bottom line. If Semco's turnover equaled the UK average of 15% per annum, and if costs per new hire were (only) $5,000, that alone would save about $2 million each year—that is, an additional $2 million profit.

# In Summary

We have traveled from Mumbai to Germany to Spain and to Brazil for examples that mimic all or part of our idealized networked model. Each illustrates in its own way the deep simplicity of such structures: independence *and* community via shared stuff.

These organizations might not receive much comment. It is hard to find the heroes and antiheroes journalists love to write about in shared leadership environments, as Senge pointed out.[7] Nevertheless, taken together, they suggest, as a recent *McKinsey Quarterly* did, it could be time to make the network the organization.[8] This might sound a little odd to the dabbawalas of Mumbai who did it 120 years ago. They might ask whether there is any other way.

# Takeaways From Chapter 9

From Mumbai and the dabbawalas, we learned the following:

- Self-organization and high quality can go together.
- New technology is not a prerequisite for networks.
- The appeal of networks might well be universal.

From Germany and the SAP Community Network, we learned the following:

- Corporations exist as part of an ecosystem.
- The ecosystem contains latent communities.
- Such communities, hosted intelligently, can offer significant business advantage.

From Spain and Mondragon we learned the following:

- There are successful alternatives to the hierarchical command-and-control model.
- There is an alternative to the unitary board system.
- A proven alternative is network governance.

From Brazil and Semco we learned the following:

- Traditional companies have considerable potential for network-like behavior.
- Offering autonomy releases higher engagement.
- Higher engagement delivers better results.

# CHAPTER 10

# The Closing Circle

At the close of a network meeting, we sit in a circle, and our discussion leader might say,

> To finish our meeting, we will pass this microphone around. You are invited to share whatever is on your mind. But it's voluntary. The only requests I make are, first, if you speak, you must have something to say; second, please say it clearly and with directness; and third, if you are listening, please do so with intention and care. This is the closing circle.

I invite you to join a virtual circle now. Already here, besides myself, are some other people whose ideas have stimulated me. We have been discussing the future of organizations.

Gary Hamel has to catch an early plane, so he speaks first. He reads from a blog he wrote recently, titled *Imperious Institutions, Impotent Individuals*, which pretty much tells you where he is coming from. Snippets of Gary's comments lodge in my mind:[1]

- There is a fault line that runs between individuals and institutions . . . a fundamental breakdown in trust.
- Trust is not simply a matter of truthfulness . . . It is also a matter of amity and goodwill. We trust those who have our best interests at heart, and mistrust those who seem deaf to our concerns.
- The misalignment is the result of . . . compensation systems that discourage long-term thinking, and of authoritarian management practices that undermine morale and frustrate contribution.

- As power moves away from the periphery and toward the center, individual influence wanes . . . The result: a population that feels aggrieved and impotent.
- I believe the Internet has also been contributing . . . We have rushed to take advantage of its . . . meritocratic structure . . . [and] become less tolerant of top down power structures.
- Whatever the cause, the data are clear: More and more of us feel that our institutions are run for the benefit of those who are leading them.

And he closes with this question: "Why can't we build organizations that are highly adaptable, endlessly inventive, and truly inspiring?"[2] Well, Gary certainly had something to say, and he said it directly.

There is a thoughtful silence as the microphone passes to Antoni Lee. Antoni is not a famous professor of management like Gary, but he is a student of thoughtful opinion. He says,

> While recovering from a minor operation recently, I reviewed *The Economist*'s predictions for the coming year. I summarized them, and sent them out as a service to my clients. Here's what I wrote about leadership . . . It complements what Gary said.[3]

*The Economist* predicts:

- New kinds of organizations: Today's hierarchical pyramid is not equipped to handle tomorrow's problems. We need a culture of trust where managers are accountable to employees.
- Bottom up leadership: Responsibility is pushed down to employees.
- Redefinition of organizational structure: Employees first, customers second.
- Companies: Those that survive will be . . . smaller, family owned, unlisted on exchanges and free of debt.
- Social networks: Will change the nature of relationships. Well-connected people are more productive, emotionally satisfied and have higher self esteem.

I can't help smiling at this as I recall that those with strong networks also live longer. This is very comforting at age 70.

Shann Turnbull is next. He is sitting next to Dee Hock. They are the governance experts in the room and have enjoyed each other's company (or at least, they have in my imagination). Shann, the academic, goes first. He says,

> These problems can be summarized briefly as: the tendency of centralized power to corrupt; the difficulty of managing complexity; and the suppression of human checks and balances. What we need now are organisations which recognize these failings and are designed to overcome them—organisations which break down complexity into manageable units, decompose organizational decision-making into a network of independent centres and allow the private interests of executives to be harnessed to the public good. Command and control hierarchies must be replaced by . . . "network governance" . . . [These] aspirations are grounded in practice, as well as theory.[4]

And if anyone made sure they were grounded in practice, it was Dee Hock, with his amazingly successful Visa experiment. His views on the failure of existing models are well known. So he injects a novel note: he picks up on Shann's key word, "governance," and expands on it on purpose, literally:

> Rules and regulations, laws and contracts, can never replace clarity of shared purpose . . . There is no way to give people purpose . . . The only possibility is to evoke the gift of self-governance from the people themselves. People everywhere are . . . desperate for a renewed sense of community . . . [and] commonly shared purpose and principles.[5]

Makes you think, doesn't it? What *is* the purpose of a business? To make a profit? I've never found that satisfying enough. We need profit like we need air to breathe. But I wouldn't say the purpose of life is the search for air. Someone once said that the purpose of a business was to find and keep customers. That's not bad. Visa's purpose was "creating the world's premier system for the exchange of value." That's better. Ours is "to help our affiliates craft the lives they want while crafting our own." Hock added it might take months to clarify your purpose—but it's worth the effort.

My mind races on: So what is wrong with the money purpose? Nothing, except when it becomes the game. And this happens so quickly, as I recall. Company headquarters sets the financial targets for the coming year. They are passed down through the levels, each adding a buffer—just in case. Finally, Bob, the branch manager in, say, Christchurch, New Zealand, gets his well-padded portion. Now the compensation and benefits team designs an incentive scheme to motivate him. Someone fires the start gun on January 1, and already, by February 7, he is in Auckland, with all the other branch managers, trying to explain that January is always quiet—it's the holidays, after all. Why don't these guys in Hong Kong (or wherever) understand that the seasons and summer vacations are back-to-front in the Southern Hemisphere? Thereafter, monthly measurement meetings continue. The managers, including Bob, soon develop the habit of always being in the office at the month's end to ensure all the numbers are counted properly, which cramps business activities and private life somewhat.

What happens to the targets if there's an economic problem? Perhaps the New Zealand dollar dives or rises, or a global financial crisis might hit. It takes time for headquarters to respond, if at all. Those guys in Hong Kong are preoccupied with China anyway. So Bob resigns himself to the game of meeting his targets *somehow*. Come year's end, who can blame him if he finds some games to play with his numbers? (He knows they do it at headquarters: Those smooth quarter-on-quarter growth numbers are the result of a special group that knows how to accelerate and delay revenue as needed. So why shouldn't he play, too?) Maybe he can persuade some of his local distributors (who are, conveniently, members of the same rugby club) to order some extra stock at year end. They understand they can return any unused models next quarter, as necessary.

I guess this is all the result of making it clear (in reality) that the whole purpose of the business is to make the numbers—the money. It's not pretty. As if he is reading my mind, Donald Curtis speaks up:

I'd like to pick up on playing the game of numbers. Therein lies the analogue management trap. Modern management . . . [is] a system of concepts and tools intended to maximize the ability of the top management group to understand, direct and control the business. At the heart of this . . . are two fundamental premises:

- The important characteristics of a business can be quantified.
- This ability . . . can be used to . . . support management activities [like] understanding, directing and controlling the enterprise.

These two premises . . . are false. [They] lead to the "analogue management trap." Analogue comes from analogy and means to represent something with something else.[6]

So the numbers aren't real? They are only an analogy? I need to think about that.

As it so happens (oh, the wonder of pulling the strings), another academic, Edward Deci, is next. Interestingly, he was once sacked from a business school faculty because of his "heretical findings about rewards." He takes up the cudgel of measurement, rewards, and control (because that's surely what rewards are for) and says,

In 1999 we analyzed three decades of studies into what motivates people. One hundred twenty-eight experiments led to the conclusion that tangible rewards tend to have a substantially negative effect on intrinsic motivation. When institutions . . . focus on the short term and opt for controlling behavior . . . They do considerable long term damage.[7]

I'm thinking "intrinsic" means "for free." That's a way to save money. I'm also thinking that if Bob's colleagues in all the other branches around the world are doing the same thing—massaging the numbers, and I'm sure many are—then long-term damage (at minimum to productivity and customer respect) is sure to happen. But it could be much worse: Maybe it means the smartest, canniest game players get the most money and the fastest promotions and are soon at the top. But isn't that what caused the global financial crisis in 2008 and 2009?

Charles Handy interrupts my reverie: He says, "We need to learn the concept of enough."[8] I'd heard him say this before in an address in Singapore. I'd thought about it and decided he was right. Is unending growth possible? I don't know the answer to that, but I decided there was some truth in his statement. And here he is repeating it. Our reaction was to sort out our purpose, agree on our deep simplicity (how we'd go about it), resolve to stay solvent, and then add a very simple measure of progress, with plenty of wiggle room, namely, to grow at around 10% per annum on average, as measured not in money but in number of clients attending our workshops. (That's meant to focus us on what is actually happening with affiliates and clients and not be distracted by currency movements and the like.) And if the business ever ran out of steam, as inevitably it must, we should find something else to do. We've been lucky. Over 20 years, we've made those objectives and made money, but not by playing games to do so, and never by offering incentives to affiliates that might lead to game playing, as all incentives do. This is light-years from what I'd been trained to do at IBM. And the strange thing is, being OK with enough, growth seemed to come more naturally, more easily. Maybe when you are naturally engaged, doing things you like doing, you are more relaxed, and the clients and affiliates notice this, and you are a more attractive organization to do business with as a result. Is that possible?

Talking about what you like doing best is the cue for Laura Roberts (of Harvard Business School, Wharton, etc.) to speak. She contributes a fable:

> The animals decided to form a school. The curriculum consisted of lessons in swimming, running, flying, climbing and jumping. At first, the duck was the best swimmer until he wore out his flippers in running class. The best runner was the dog, but he crash-landed in flying class and broke his leg. The rabbit excelled at jumping until he injured his back after falling in climbing class. The school dux was the eel. She could do a little of everything, but nothing really well.[9]

She concluded with the advice to create a place where people can use their strengths. This makes sense to me. I suppose that's the end of the performance review, which always focused on what you can't do well. (Anyway, we've never conducted one in 20 years, as you can't do that in a network.) Warm smiles greeted Laura's charming way of making a serious point.

My turn with the microphone is coming up. What will I choose to say in a minute or less? Will I recap the thesis of this book, like this?

> We started from the opposite pole to big institutions. It turns out some of them are now heading toward the same place, but from the opposite direction. This is where we encounter the following— not always, but often enough to excite us:
>
> - There is a certain dignity that is associated with a person who takes control of her own life.
> - When that control is aligned with a sense of purpose that fulfils her, pleases others, and does not harm the environment, and when it allows her to exploit her signature strengths, we observe a certain artistic quality in work and life.
> - If two such people connect and discover shared stuff, collaboration and mutual support seem natural.
> - Discovering others with similar mind-sets lays the foundation for community.
> - As this community links with other, complementary communities, something akin to a cooperative, or a coalition, emerges.
> - All this is built on respect, autonomy, collaboration, trust, and signature strengths. The catalysts are hosts and shared leadership.
> - This organization is often innovative and resilient—a place within which members can craft their lives, suitable to them, their season, and their strengths.

Just rehearsing this in my mind reminds me of my many seasons so far. My present one I describe as graceful degradation. When I started my business career, my objective was to retire at 55. That would be success: getting out early. It sounds like getting out of jail when I write it now. Today, however, I want to keep working. That means reflecting, writing, mentoring, traveling, starting a new business, and enjoying our annual family migrations to the beach and snow. I'm healthy, happy, and lucky.

I enjoy the company of a wide network of colleagues and friends. Research says this will, on average, extend my life.[10] I'm working and playing and getting more years to do it all in. Who would want to stop?

Talking about playing, the graphics I've used in this book were dreamed up while sailing from Tahiti to New Zealand. Should I use my minute to review those in the closing circle? Like this?

> We started with the importance of the connection. We contrasted two and represented them like this, in Figure 10.1.
>
> We then added more connections to establish a simple hub-and-spoke network, like in Figure 10.2.
>
> Connecting the affiliates led to a community, as shown in Figure 10.3.
>
> And, finally, we have a coalition of communities in Figure 10.4.

But no, if you have faithfully read the whole book, you don't need me to repeat these. Maybe the best way to use my minute is to recount a story that sums up all these ideas. When I look up from my reverie, you and everyone else have been waiting patiently for me to decide what to say:

> Something quite moving happened at our Brussels network meeting; something that spoke to the formation of community at a deep level. An 18-year-old woman present had been assaulted in a foreign city while working there as an English teacher. Fortunately,

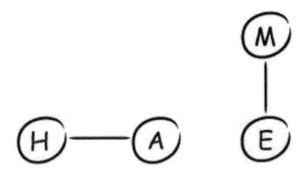

*Figure 10.1. The contrast.*

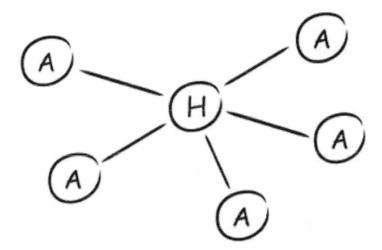

*Figure 10.2. Connections.*

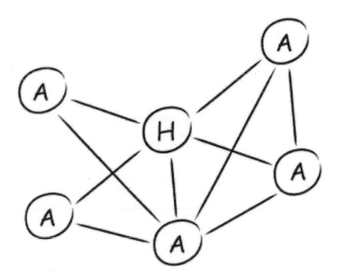

*Figure 10.3. Community.*

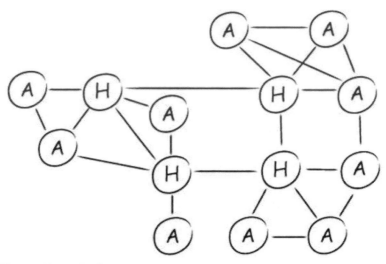

*Figure 10.4. Coalition.*

she frightened her attacker away. Nevertheless, she was devastated by the experience. Over lunch one day, she felt this was a safe place to share such a matter with some of the other women. Mysteriously, the next day, a new option appeared on the Open Space agenda: a session on practical self-defense. It was offered by an expert present. Nearly half of the 35 people attended, and none of them, except the leader (and the young lady, I suspect), knew what triggered it.

At the time of the closing circle, the young woman was not present. When it came to my turn, as now, I commented that friendship, community, even love were evident in this initiative. I confess my eyes were moist, and I had some difficulty speaking. The woman who'd been attacked was my own daughter. You met her earlier as a 5-year-old.

Even the possibility that an item like this could emerge in a network meeting signals to me, at least, real community. It would now be difficult to return to traditional agendas, traditional authority, and traditional structures.

The network is the organization of the future.

The session leader quietly invites us all to stand, to look around the circle, and to acknowledge each other, what we have accomplished, and what we hope to do. After a minute or so, she asks us to turn around and look out of the circle and to reflect for a moment on what we will do as a result of our time together. I resolve to write a book. What have you decided to do? Finally, we say our good-byes and leave.

Good-bye.

And thank you for our conversations.

# RESOURCE 1

# Money Is Thin;
# Life Is Thick

People work for money, right? Well, apparently it's not that simple. Recent insights about extrinsic (external) versus intrinsic (internal) motivation call the money assumption (or money-only assumption) into question. Our experience confirms this. This chapter explores the following questions:

- What is money?
- What else motivates people?
- How does this work in real life?

## What Is Money?

I admit to being ignorant about money for most of my life. I naïvely thought it was something printed or pressed by official government agencies. Then I met Roland Spinola. He invited me to conferences on complementary currencies and suggested readings that allowed me to lose my innocence in the safety of my own home. I learned that, yes, the government does produce some money but that there are other money producers, too—notably the banks, who lend more than they have in their vaults as credit, thereby creating purchasing power, or money.

I also learned this practice started with dishonest goldsmiths.[1] It seems that in the late Middle Ages, gold and silver coins were the main form of money. If you had more of these than was safe to leave in your house, you could deposit them with the local goldsmith, the only person with a reliable strong room. He would give you a receipt in return. Over time, you could pass on this receipt in payment for something rather than withdraw your coins, which is why my checks today still read, "or bearer."

Some sharp goldsmith noticed that he always had some coins left in his vault, so he decided to notionally borrow some of them, issue receipts, and lend these on interest. This practice became the basis for how banks lend funds, although today there is some supervision by central banks.

Upon learning all this, I began to see money in an entirely new light. I learned of other types of currencies—salt was once a currency, as were clam shells and wheat. I learned about local currencies, such as the *Wirtschafsring* ("economic circle") of companies in Switzerland, and even a time currency in Japan, about which a small diversion.

*Hureai kippu* is Japanese for "caring relationship tickets." It is a currency designed to help the rapidly aging Japanese population. The unit of account is an hour of service. If, for example, you help an elderly neighbor do his shopping, you earn credits based on the number of hours you contribute. These accumulate. You can keep them in your account for when you get sick or old or transfer them to someone else. For example, you might give them to your elderly father in another city. You create value simply by giving your time. This is very emancipating. If I give up an hour or two of television viewing, I can create value. This makes both economic and human sense. There is a bonus for the elderly, too: They prefer the care provided by the people who work for *hureai kippu* over those who are paid normally in yen.

What's the point of all this? My certainties about money were shaken. If the sources of money are many, not backed by real coins or notes or gold, or even produced by governments, then money is simply a construct—often very useful, but only a construct. Today, money is reduced to bits and bytes.

When Donald Curtis said accounting is only an analogue (i.e., another construct), my head began to spin. We are now two steps removed from reality—whatever that is. He spoke out strongly:

Companies fall into the analogue management trap by making three fundamental errors:

- Believing . . . measurements are . . . more accurate than is actually possible
- Believing . . . they can therefore control . . . and manage the underlying *business activities*

- Not understanding that managing through analogues is self-fulfilling[2]

What is an analogue? It's something that purports to measure something else. Think of it like the speedometer in your car. It reflects your speed, but it is not speed—it's an analogue for it. Moving the needle is not the point: This can even be done without moving the car, as some sharp businesses have demonstrated. The speedometer offers feedback, and like most analogues, the information it offers is thin. It conveys nothing about what it feels like to be going fast in a sports car with the top down. The latter is a thick, multisensory experience. Likewise, money is thin while life is thick.

It is undeniably difficult for large, public companies to avoid the focus on money. Their results are scrutinized by the press, the investment community, and the shareholders. However, some of the financial speedometer readings are arbitrary or, at least, imprecise. Just as a student's performance can be expressed in a number, or an alphabetic grade, it depends on who is doing the grading. And sometimes grades are weighted for effort rather than performance.

The bottom line for me was that money is no longer an absolute and reliable measure of anything (e.g., a liter of water) and an even less reliable indicator of how we are going about crafting a life. I now felt free (as long as we were solvent) to explore other currencies.

## What Else Motivates People?

As Pink notes, the research says that while money incentives might help for unattractive work, what really motivates people are intrinsic motivators, variously described as "competence, autonomy, and relatedness"[3] or "autonomy, mastery, and purpose."[4] We independently came up with independence, community, and shared stuff. There is lots of overlap here. I suspect there are even more intrinsic motivators—like happiness, perhaps.

A study called "Money, Sex and Happiness: An Empirical Study" published in the *Scandinavian Journal of Economics* explores this.[5] The paper quotes a survey correlating 19 work-life factors and happiness. The lowest correlation, the thing that bugs people the most about work, is commuting. I note in passing that working away from an office is a feature of Results-Only Work Environment (ROWE) organizations and networks.

So if commuting correlates most negatively with happiness, what is the most positive correlate? Well, it's sex (or more sex). In the group of 12,000 workers who were polled, regular sex with a regular partner correlated highest of all, and higher than money. The researchers computed how much more you'd need to earn to match the happiness produced by more frequent sex. Sex once a week rather than once a month was the equivalent of $50,000 additional income. There are more currencies than money.

## How Does This Work in Real Life?

I suggest there is a large variety of such currencies, and they vary by individual and over time. Few who take up our kind of business do so for money only. You might recall Fitzy, who went to India for "excitement, challenge, and a modest income." Here are a few more examples.

### Mothering

Hiah was a client-cum-business partner when I invited her to a Think on Your Feet Network (TOYFNET) meeting in Palmerston North, New Zealand. She was in charge of senior executive–development programs for one of Singapore's government-owned investment companies— the company that owns large chunks of Singapore Airlines, Singapore Technologies, and so forth. We'd enjoyed a partnership offering TOYF together, and I liked the way she did business. On a whim, which I still can't quite explain, I asked if she'd like to join us in New Zealand. I guess I thought her unique insider-outsider perspective gave her insights we could all benefit from.

One exercise we did there was to create a model for where we were now and where we wanted to be in 2 years' time. We then explained it to our colleagues and listened to their ideas. Most of the differences fell into the work-life balance equation that so preoccupies businesses today.

Hiah explained her situation: She had a good job, she didn't need to work, but she wanted to. But most of all she wanted more time for her children, who were just starting school. She wanted to support them through their formative years. But what she didn't want was to be stuck at home without being involved in something else. She also valued her independence. I recall her saying she liked having the freedom to buy things, like her own clothing. It was symbolic of being in charge of her life.

The more she spoke, the more I could see we could use her experience—and possibly pay enough for her clothes. She could work part time and any hours she wished. We needed help in Singapore (as I had just moved to London). I made my suggestion, and she accepted, to my delight.

Thirteen years later, her eldest (now 19) has qualified to enter a prestigious college in London; another has been a Singapore national sports representative, and so on. Hiah has focused on her role as mother: running her kids to school and sports, making sure they learned Chinese as well as English, acting as manager for the international sports team her daughter was on, and more. She has her own company and is a director of ours. Meanwhile, her husband has been elected managing partner of his professional firm, and Hiah travels extensively with him doing her part in this new role.

Recently, we had the chance to reminisce. I congratulated her on bringing up her children so well—and meeting the goals she set for herself 13 years ago. I said, "Will you want to stop working with us now?" "Not at all," she replied. "You originally offered me freedom and independence. But I'm not resigning, if that's OK, because now you give me identity." I was taken aback. "What do you mean?" She replied, "I am not just XYZ's mother or ABC's wife. I am also regional director for KEI [Ken Everett International P/L], and I run my own company. My friends who only have the roles conferred by their husbands and children are jealous." I didn't know we were offering identity. That's a very valuable currency, which is just as well because I doubt we pay her enough. Clearly, we've had the opportunity to help Hiah craft her life. Clearly she's helped us craft ours. And clearly, she works for reasons that are thicker than money.

### Fathering

Peter, my son and business partner, aims to eat with his young family (an 8-year-old daughter and a 6-year-old son) each night. This is much earlier than most Sydney executives leave their offices, let alone get home. This doesn't mean he can't return to his home office after putting them to bed or that he can't make an occasional trip away. It's just that these are the exceptions. This is worth a lot of money to him and his wife. Her friends are jealous of her, too.

### Grandparenting

Today, in my 70s, excursions by our extended family have first priority in my calendar. During my 60s, I spent heavily in time and money to expand our international coverage. I'll do less of this in my 70s. I can focus on consolidating our various startups, as well as on the grandchildren. My planning period is thus in decades, not months or even a year. Annual profit results are too thin to reveal this level of strategy. I am trying to craft my life, too.

If this way of seeing things suggests other pathways to rewarding work, higher engagement, reduced turnover, and happier staff—and continues to outperform the command and control models—then perhaps investors will learn to favor such organizations. Perhaps we should have analogues for independence, mastery, and purpose, and it seems we have: "Engagement" is the term du jour.

For Hiah, the independence to build her work life around her children for 13 years, the mastery of parenting this offered her, and her purpose (the family outcomes she desired) was engagement of a very high order, and her role with us enabled all this. The word "engagement" sounds too thin in her case. How about "dedication"?

Whatever the right word is, we seem to have it in networks, in hybrid organizations like Wikipedia and Mozilla, and in the ROWEs and in companies like Semco (chapter 9),[6] too. They have all tapped into something thicker than money as an incentive.

## Takeaways From Resource 1

- Money is a construct.
- The accounts are analogues.
- Extrinsic rewards can work for unattractive work.
- Intrinsic rewards are more motivating.

- These rewards include independence, community, purpose, and more.
- Networks offer the freedom to enjoy these rewards.
- Other organizations can adapt to emphasize these rewards, too.
- The result is the ability to craft a life.
- Evidence suggests these advantages are reciprocated.
- Money is thin; life is thick.

# RESOURCE 2

# Affiliate Profile

The initial conversation with a prospective affiliate will range over a number of things, including how they met us, why they are interested, what they do in their business, who their typical clients are, and much more. Beyond that, we always make sure we cover the following, which I've organized as initial discovery, business compatibility, and contractual stuff.

## Initial Discovery

We look for three key things in a relationship with an affiliate:

1. *Trust*
   a. Because we deal across distance
   b. Because we deal in intellectual property
   c. Because we want to capture the economies of trust in doing business
   d. How do you feel about this?
2. *Collaborative mindset*
   a. Are you open to working collaboratively with other affiliates in the same marketplace?
   b. Are you open to working with affiliates globally?
   c. If so, there are opportunities for synergy.
3. *Business skills*
   a. Can you sell, or do you work with someone who can?
   b. Can you facilitate, or do you work with someone who can?
   c. What else do you bring to the table?
   d. Can you survive the first year?
   e. Who are your clients? What is your track record?

## Business Compatibility

We like to understand the what, where, when, why, and how of your business, your plans for our products, and your plans for your business as a whole.

We like to see that we're compatible. Will we fit well together? Will you complement the network we've created?

We'd like to help you craft your future. If we can do that, and you can help us craft ours, then we have a good match.

## Contractual Stuff

We ask you to sign a standard affiliate contract covering territory, term, and so forth.

Among other things, the contract sets out to do the following:

- Protect the intellectual property.
- Protect the brand.
- Ensure quality in delivery.
- Ensure reasonable product consistency worldwide (important to multinational clients).
- Ensure we deal with everyone equally.

We think these requirements are in your interests, as well as ours.

# RESOURCE 3

# Research Project

## How Do Networks Work?

Between 2008 and 2010, we researched some answers to this question. Here we describe that project and its outcomes:

- What is the background to the research?
- How was it conducted?
- What were the conclusions?
- What else is noteworthy?

## What Is the Background to the Research?

1. *The setting.* In May 2008, we held our first network-to-network (N2N) meeting in Gualdo, Italy. This coalition of networks was represented earlier, as in Figure 13.1. At the 2008 meeting, there was a mixture of hubs and affiliates. The latter came for a variety of reasons. Some were thinking about becoming hubs based on their own intellectual property. Others were interested in connecting with more hubs for possible business relationships. A few simply enjoyed the exchange of stimulating ideas in a rustic Italian environment.

2. *The person.* Adina Luca brought a unique set of perspectives to this meeting. She had been an affiliate of the Think on Your Feet Network (TOYFNET), helping to set us up in her native Romania. (Her company was recommended to us by a client.) Later, Adina joined a client organization and experienced that perspective. She then became associated with another network, the ITIM (intercultural management) network, a culture and management consultancy. She turned this interest into a specific study on Romanian management culture, and published her findings in *Employeescu*.[1] This sparked

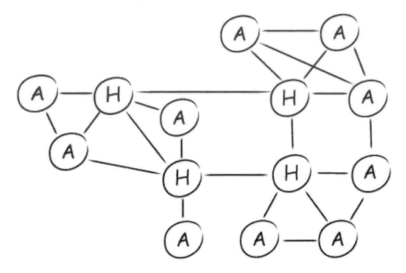

*Figure 13.1. An N2N network.*

her interest in research. Recently, Adina has started a small, new consultancy based on business analytics. Thus Adina represents several of the projected membership types for an expanded N2N, as suggested earlier and shown in Figure 13.2.

3. *The question.* How do networked organizations work?

## How Was the Research Conducted?

The topic was explored with hubs in semistructured interviews via these questions:

- How does the network you are a part of work?
- How do others become members of your network and why?
- What makes the members of your network stay a part of the network?
- What are successful practices in your network and why?
- What are unsuccessful practices in your network and why?

Adina made the following observation in her report to us:

The methodology I used for this project was a qualitative research method, Grounded Theory. The Grounded Theory was appropriate

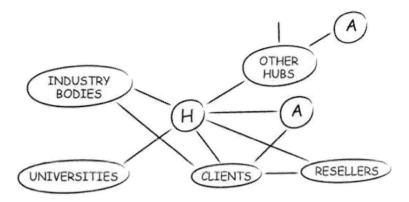

*Figure 13.2. An extended N2N network.*

because it allowed for the analysis of the research participants' experience, who met the criteria of leading / managing network hubs, and was not abstractly derived. The views collected from seven research participants via semi-structured in-depth interviews were analysed for thematic content and the themes were logically structured to form a theory of the subject.[2]

The participants in the research were from the networks listed in Table 13.1.

## What Were the Conclusions?

Adina identified in the design of most networks three common processes:

1. The people process, which describes how affiliates come to be affiliates
2. The hub process, which describes how the hub manages or influences some of the risks inherent in the design, like internal competition and communication (or lack of it)
3. The market process, which describes how affiliates go to market and how each maximizes their individual results

Specifically, all interviewees agreed on the following:

- The hub needs to provide startup support.

*Table 13.1.  Research Participant Networks*

| Name of network | Country of origin or hub | Age | Size (no. affiliates) | Countries with network membership |
|---|---|---|---|---|
| Barnes & Conti | United States | 25 years | 43 | 15 countries: United States, Canada, United Kingdom, Germany, France, Poland, Hungary, Lithuania, Israel, Chile, Mexico, China, Singapore, Australia, Japan |
| Hermann International (HBDI) | Asia: Australia | 20 years | 450 | 11 countries: Australia, New Zealand, China, Japan, South Korea, Singapore, Malaysia, United Arab Emirates, India, Hong Kong, Philippines |
| | Central Europe: Germany | 22 years | 850 | 3 countries: Germany, Austria, Switzerland |
| IOWEU | Hong Kong | 3 years | 90 | 21 countries: Australia, Austria, Belgium, Canada, China, France, Germany, Ireland, Italy, The Netherlands, Poland, Romania, Hong Kong, Singapore, South Africa, South Korea, Spain, Switzerland, Thailand, United Kingdom, United States |
| ITIM International | The Netherlands | 25 years | 60 | 23 countries: Norway, Sweden, Denmark, Germany, Poland, Czech Republic, Netherlands, Switzerland, Belgium, France, Italy, Spain, Portugal, Greece, Turkey, India, China, Australia, Argentina, Mexico, United States, United Kingdom, Brazil |
| Passion Works! | Canada | 4 years | 25 | 11 countries: Canada, United States, United Kingdom, Bermuda, Malaysia, Belgium, Singapore, Hong Kong, Korea, Thailand, Vietnam |
| TOYFNET | Australia | 19 years | 120 | 30 countries: Australia, Canada, United States, France, United Kingdom, Italy, Germany, Romania, Poland, Ireland, Cyprus, Russia, Belarus, Kazakhstan, Ukraine, Switzerland, Belgium, Singapore, Hong Kong, Indonesia, China, Japan, Taiwan, South Korea, Malaysia, United Arab Emirates, Kuwait, India, New Zealand, Thailand |

- This support includes investing in the startup costs or assisting with first sales.

Most interviewees agreed on the following:

- The hub does not need to offer territorial exclusivity.
- The hub needs to foster collaboration and pay attention to potential internal competition among affiliates.
- The hub needs to build layers of membership to support regional growth.
- Affiliates will vary widely in their levels of activity.
- Affiliates leave a network via self-elimination rather than any other process.

Expanding on these conclusions, Adina observed the following characteristics:

- The product and pricing are variables that do not shape the networked organization; in other words, the hub cannot use the product and pricing as levers to advance its objectives of growth. The hub's levers are the quality of relationships that it has established with the affiliates and the marketplace.
- In contrast to the traditional organization, the values of the networked organization are community-building values and not performance drivers; moreover, the hub is restricted in building a certain set of values as they are inherent in the selection process of affiliates—that is, only people with certain types of values are attracted to this type of organization.
- Although the hub may seem at times redundant and easy to dispose of because the affiliates are able to fend for themselves and replicate the networked organization someplace else, the hub is in fact essential because it regulates two processes that are essential for the organization: the internal competition and the communication channels.

Adina continues,

In essence, a networked organization is a relationship organization. To build such an organization, the hub needs to

1.  Facilitate the relationships among affiliates and connectors in the marketplace,
2.  Regulate internal competition and host the affiliates' communication, and
3.  Explore market opportunities through outside connections in order to facilitate the success of affiliates.

While it sounds very simple, this model requires an ability that covers a lot more complexity than any other ability. Sometimes it is easier . . . to write a set of procedures than to manage the conflict between two people. Moreover, there is the diversity inherent in any international business, the affiliates' characteristics—a high need for freedom and independence and a low tolerance for rules and regulations—and the internal competition that is created by the design of the networked organization. This is why these organizations are sometimes more successful if they concentrate on facilitating the community building of the affiliates and leave out (or to another entity) the product updates and other "technical" stuff.

## Additional Comments

*   This research is based on six networks, not just TOYFNET.
*   When the results were presented to the (largely) new 2010 N2N group, their responses resonated with Adina's conclusions.
*   The research is ongoing and will extend to identifying what affiliates expect from the hub and what makes a successful affiliate.
*   Further information about this research can be obtained directly as follows: Adina Luca (adina.luca@stillae.com).
*   Most comforting, all the networks that participated in the research are still active after two of the worst business years in memory. This is some kind of comment on the resilience of the networked organization.

# RESOURCE 4

# Case Study

Here is your chance to design a networked organization and to see if any of the models and how-tos in this book help you to do so.

Let's work with the organization that connects me, the author, with you, the reader. It is Business Expert Press (BEP), the publisher of this book.

The traditional business of publishing is facing challenges today. BEP has developed an innovative alternative. It seeks to connect several communities. These include authors (both academics and practitioners), course instructors, and students, to name a few. The books and their digital versions are available in collections and digital libraries. For more, see http://www.businessexpertpress.com.

BEP is clearly networked. You are a consultant at Network Designs, consultants in networked organizations. The founder of BEP, David Parker, has asked you to suggest how, if at all, you think BEP could develop as a networked organization for the benefit of all concerned.

Here are a few questions to trigger your thinking:

- What is unique about BEP's business model?
- Who benefits from that, apart from BEP?
- What are the communities BEP serves apart from authors and readers?
- What, in your view, are the keys to BEP's future success?
- How can a networked organization help with these?
- Which, if any, of the advantages of networked organizations claimed in this book might be attractive to BEP?
- If you do not recommend building a networked organization, what are your reasons, and what alternatives would you suggest?

- If you do recommend building such an organization, what communities should BEP seek to host and how?
- Are there any natural partners for network-to-network activities?

Your report to David Parker should be no longer than 10 pages, or 15 PowerPoint slides.

# RESOURCE 5

# Network Voice

Often underestimated and widely underutilized is the power of voice. Get it wrong and people will see you as a corporate heavyweight. Get it right and you can build respect, trust, and goodwill: in short, the social capital underpinning a network relationship.

In an oversimplification to make the point, let's imagine two voices: hierarchy voice and network voice, and then let's look at the following:

- Why two voices?
- What's the difference?
- When does it matter?
- What makes for good network voice?

## Why Two Voices?

The short answer is depicted in Figure 15.1.

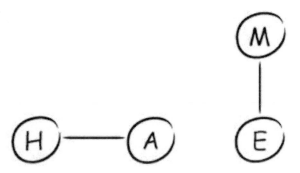

*Figure 15.1.* *The manager-employee and hub-affiliate relationships contrasted.*

## What's the Difference?

There are many archetypes for hierarchy voice: parents, teachers, coaches, and the military. It is the voice of authority. It tells us, "Attention!" "Be quiet." "You can do better." "Listen up." "Look at me."

In corporate speak, these are more politely expressed but retain their undisguised authority. "Rise for the chairman." "Your attention, please." "Growth is #1 priority for all staff." "Must read: important new information." Or "the spotlight shines on the CEO," which shows voice is not always spoken.

The archetypes for network voice are more equal: neighbors, cousins, colleagues, alumni, classmates—all kinds of fellow travelers.

In network speak, these come out as follows: "How do you do so-and-so?" "Would you like to go with me?" "How about coffee on Friday?" "What do you think about . . . ?" "Can you help me?" "Can I help you?" Note the questions versus the statements.

For clarity, we've made the contrast strong here, and to be sure, a lot depends on context, which makes the early exchanges most important because there is no agreed relationship context as yet.

## When Does It Matter?

When does it matter which voice is used? The short answer is pretty much always because a network is built on social capital.

The slightly longer answer is in all the following forms of communication:

- E-mails
- Phone calls
- Face-to-face conversations

### E-Mails

Have you ever received e-mails that sound like this?

To all country marketing managers:
The leadership team has been strategizing re the new paradigm of e-training. It's paramount we are proactive in this new space in all

geographics. From the first of next month, we will roll out our initiatives in this area, going global and acting local at the same time. This new focus will provide opportunities for our clients, our company, and you.

This is a confidential heads-up. Going forward we will keep you in the loop on the deployment details.

Let's make this innovation work for all.

R. L. (Bob) Smith
President, Product Initiatives

This kind of e-mail is full of buzzwords, corporate speak, and of course, top-down speak, telling people what will happen, making assumptions, and expecting people to follow the leader.

Maybe there is nothing wrong with this in corporate terms, but one wonders at the reception this note will get. Here's a network voice alternative:

Hello John,
Remember you said we need to update our range when I visited last month? Well, I asked around, and others feel the same way. It seems we need to do something about electronic delivery.

Would you be willing to join a small task force on this? I have in mind yourself representing Asia, Pierre for Europe, and for North America, Tony in Toronto.

If you are up for this, let me know, and if so, when in the first week of next month would be good for a joint Skype call?

In the meantime, if you want to check out how Pierre or Tony feels about this, then by all means do so.

Regards,
Bob


### Phone Calls

When making phone calls, consider the following:

- Who decides when?
- Who decides what?
- Who decides how?

When?

When to make phone calls is especially important in international calls. What time of day is it for them? Do they have family, commuting, prayer, or other rituals associated with certain times of the day? For example, Fitzy, in India, teaches a lot—which rules him out during the day. But at 5:30 p.m. he is often in transit to his home, to a hotel, or to the airport by taxi and happy to take a call on his mobile phone. Jeremy in China regularly works 6 days a week (sometimes more). Drive time works for him, too.

There are other aspects of when. Consider the following before calling:

- Days of the week worked in the Middle East are different to the United Kingdom, the United States, and Australia: It may already be tomorrow in New Zealand.
- Lunchtime is special in some countries: *A l'una* (1:00 p.m.) might not be so good in Italy.
- Consider the time difference: The laid-back end of the day for you might be high-energy, deadline-driven morning for them.
- Seasons and latitudes vary: Imagine you are there when you call; it might be snowing where you are but 120°F (50°C) in Dubai. Keep this in mind. Is the Southern Hemisphere enjoying summer break while you are skiing?
- Consider cultural festivals: Chinese New Year, Japanese New Year (and the ritual cleaning of the office that takes place before it), Yom Kippur, Friday prayers in Muslim countries, Ramadan, and so on. Show understanding of these.

What?

What will you be discussing? Maybe canvass the topic first in an e-mail and say you'd like to get input when you call. That's if you initiate.

Even so, allow for the possibility that the person you are calling might have something on their mind, too, and ask what else we should cover so you can prepare as well.

How?

How will you make the call? Skype, office line, home line, mobile? Ask them if they have a preference. If it's a conference call, learn how to set it up. About the agenda, at the very least make some notes to yourself and check at the beginning of the call that these are OK and what the other participants would like to add.

### Face-to-Face Conversations

Face-to-face conversations vary enormously, but here's the way we set up one this week:

Hi John and Phil,
I thought it might be good to swap expectations for May 9.

Pete and I hope to be briefed on where you are now (business model, needs, etc.) and where you hope to be in 2 years' time (ambitions, both personal and business). We would then know how best to help you get where you want. And how about we do the same? You may be in a position to help us as well. I imagine this will be a good investment for all of us.

If a funding scheme is necessary or desirable either way, this will emerge. But if it doesn't, we are still OK to collaborate as above.

How do you feel about these aims?

Ken

The reply we received was as follows:

Friends,
We fully share those aims and like the reciprocity.

It is open and allows many possibilities and discoveries.

All the best from Copenhagen,

Phil and John

When we meet, the conversation will follow these simple guidelines.

For network meetings, voice is also important—especially in giving the affiliates a voice. (See chapter 5 on how to make conversations the central part of the meeting.) Every now and then you need to have tough conversations, but even they can be done as naturally as possible.

## What Makes for Good Network Voice?

The following make for effective network voice:

- Avoid boss language: Remember the equality of the relationship.
- Use more questions than statements.
- Adapt to the other's time, seasons, festivals, and so forth.
- Agree mutual agendas: There should be no ambushes.
- Be natural: Don't be afraid to inject your personality.
- Listen, be genuine, be consultative, be friendly, and be professional.
- Treat the affiliate as an intelligent person with opinions.
- Act on collective opinion whenever possible.
- Be inclusive: A network is leader-full, so allow this to emerge.
- Admit mistakes when you make them: Humility goes a long way.
- Have *important* e-mails edited for tone and language by a colleague before you send them. This has been invaluable for Peter and me working as a tag team. When it's really important to get your voice right, have someone else check for you.
- Avoid corporate speak and buzzwords.

All of this can be summed up as follows:

- Respect the equality in the hub-and-affiliate relationship.
- Respect the shared stuff.
- Display empathy.

As a result you'll build very high levels of trust and amazing goodwill, and that ultimately flows through to the clients.

By the way, the points listed are good guidelines for voice in all kinds of businesses. But in networks, it is especially important not to send confusing messages about the relationship—which rests almost solely on social capital.

To conclude, here's a true story about how getting the voice right went wrong, as told by an affiliate who was listening in:

> Amongst the businessmen taking breakfast at the Crowne Plaza Hotel, Singapore, two sat near me discussing business strategy, quite loudly. One was fairly obviously a first-time visitor whose accent sounded Dutch. He was a Director from HQ. The other was the local distributor, who had lived in Singapore for many years.
>
> The distributor bubbles forth about his ideas for the local market. The visitor's objections show his impatience (and maybe jetlag?). Finally, the Director interrupts and points out that all the things being talked about have already been decided in Holland. With obvious annoyance, he points out that he has brought with him a well-thought-out plan. The best engineering input has gone into the design of the new products. Marketing has developed a strategy they are sure will be a winner. Finance has decided the pricing. With these words, "We know what we are doing. There is no need to change it," he insists the distributor does as he is told.
>
> The Director then realizes his voice has carried over the entire restaurant. In the awkward silence that follows, the two nibble at their food. After a couple of minutes, the local summarizes: "So, as I hear it, you want me to carry out this plan to the letter, to confine my activities to the market segments you specify, not to modify the specs in any way and to report monthly in the format provided. Have I got it right?" The Director smiles in confirmation and relief.
>
> "I thought you might say that," says the distributor. "So, I've brought you a present. It might be too late to save your company, but it may help you personally in the future. Oh, and by the way, you will need to find a new Singapore distributor."
>
> With that, he walks thoughtfully from the restaurant. The Director is embarrassed to be the center of attention. To divert himself, he opens the present. It is a book. I am close enough to see the cover. I know it well.
>
> It is *Maverick* by Ricardo Semler.[1]

# RESOURCE 6

# About Us

This resource is for those curious about the following:

- Our product
- Our long-term business performance
- The contributors to this book
- How we can continue the conversation

## What Is Our Product?

In one sense our product is the network. In another sense, the products we offer—via the network—cover a range of communications skills. The best known is Think on Your Feet (TOYF). What does it do?

Knowledge workers work with ideas. They explain, propose, and defend their ideas in written and verbal form. Verbal communication is sometimes formal, sometimes informal. For formal communication, presentation skills is a near-universal offering in corporate curricula. For informal communication, there is TOYF. And 90% of verbal communication is informal. That is, it is spontaneous, on the spot, and in the moment. The question is: How do you convey your ideas with clarity and economy when unrehearsed? This is the challenge TOYF addresses.[1]

TOYF has Canadian roots. The author, Keith Spicer, PhD, was a Canadian academic, author, editor, and television host, as well as Canada's first official languages commissioner. He grew up in an intellectual atmosphere redolent with the ideas of Marshall McLuhan, who was famous for coining the phrases "the global village" and "the medium is the message." McLuhan positioned Canada at the forefront of communication theory and practice.

When Keith became editor of the *Ottawa Citizen* he let go of his baby, TOYF. Roger HB Davies stepped forward, as his company McLuhan &

Davies is a Toronto-based communications skills training house. Davies had the foresight to see TOYF as an embryonic classic and acquired the rights. That was in 1985. We became involved in 1991, starting in Australia and New Zealand, then Asia, and finally, Europe.[2]

## What Is Our Long-Term Business Performance?

We consider the best measure of our business performance to be the number of people who attend our workshops. This does not directly reflect financial performance, but it is close. Financial performance is clouded by exchange-rate movements (we do business in six currencies), pricing, and other things. We have made a profit in every year and regard the financial management of the business as important but fundamentally second to customer acceptance.

Figure 16.1 reflects an underlying growth in customer acceptance over 20 years. This, in turn, is based on affiliate growth and geographic expansion. It also shows vividly how we rise and fall on the economic tides. Note the impact, in turn, of the following:

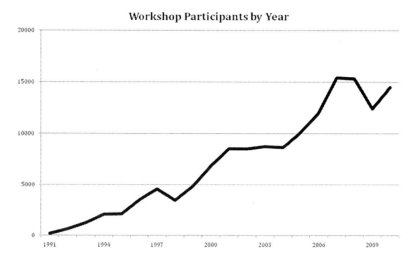

*Figure 16.1. Business performance over 20 years.*

- The 1997 Asian financial crisis
- September 11, 2001
- Severe acute respiratory syndrome in 2003 and 2004
- The global financial crisis in 2008 and 2009

Underlying these effects is a pleasing, long-term growth pattern.

## Who Are Our Contributors?

There are many—throughout the Think on Your Feet Network (TOYF-NET) and beyond. But five have helped especially in the preparation of this book:

- Richard White
- Jacqueline Throop-Robinson
- Roland Spinola
- Adina Luca
- Peter Everett

### Richard White

Richard is the lead trainer in Europe for TOYF. He is also a musician with a passion for collecting vintage saxophones.

Ric's corporate career spans engineering, customer service, marketing, and sales in the telecom industry. As a result, he is acutely aware of the need for real value in ideas and is rightly questioning of pure theory. He helps others develop their skills in communications, thinking, and creativity.

Ric enjoys the respect of our European (indeed international) network. As a result, when I returned to Australia, he acted on our behalf for several years. He is also coauthor (with Jacqueline and me) of Deep Simplicity, a workshop on networking and complexity. During the research for Deep Simplicity, Ric developed an interest in complexity and, in particular, the phenomenon of emergence at the edge of chaos.

He researched this in a novel way: He invited a group of performing artists (other musicians, dancers, painters, and poets) to join him in creating purely novel performances. No rehearsals were conducted. Minimal starting instructions were shared. The performances started and then emerged as novel works of art based on the interactions between all forms of expression present. His work in this area continues.

As an engineer, musician, collector, facilitator, and experimenter, Ric has always been pushing our thinking in both creative and disciplined ways.

### Jacqueline Throop-Robinson

Jacqueline is the cofounder of Breakthrough Learning Inc. and Passion-Works! Inc. Her own passions include her family (two young children and her life partner, Evan), the fine arts (in which she has a master's degree), and her work.

Her work focuses on shared leadership. What distinguishes her approach is the way she combines support for individual needs and business goals. Her overwhelming experience is that when the two are aligned, momentum and results are inevitable.

Jacqueline is also the hub of the PassionWorks! network, with affiliates in North America, Asia, and Europe. And as mentioned previously, we codeveloped Deep Simplicity. We share an interest, therefore, in both the theory and the practice of network building.

Notably, Jacqueline led the exploration of meeting formats within TOYFNET. For example, she introduced both Open Space and The World Café. The repeat attendance at our meetings has improved significantly as a result.

Jacqueline is a superb facilitator of groups, which places her in high demand for change management, strategic planning, leadership development, coaching, communication skills, creative thinking, problem solving, conflict management, and decision making. She continues to research passion at work, network science, and shared leadership.

The cocaring support of her life partner means Jacqueline can continue to indulge her passion for cross-cultural work. She has worked in North America, Singapore, Malaysia, Hong Kong, Japan, Australia, United Kingdom, Romania, Italy, Malta, Brazil, the Caribbean, and Bermuda.

### Roland Spinola

Michael Morgan of the Herrmann Asia network introduced me to Roland in a singularly helpful example of network-to-network (N2N) activity. We quickly discovered many commonalities in our past—including long careers in IBM. Roland was born and raised in Cologne, Germany. He worked at IBM for 24 years since 1966, both in Germany and internationally.

In 1990 he founded the Herrmann Institut Deutschland, the representative of Herrmann International for the German-speaking countries. After our first face-to-face meeting in 1999 (in Dublin of all places), Roland agreed to help us launch TOYF in Germany. His brother, Axel, a professional translator, translated our materials.

Roland has long been captivated by the growing problems in our financial systems. He infected me with his interest, invited me to conferences on the topic, and introduced me to Bernard Lietaer. Lietaer's work demonstrates why networks are so resilient (see chapter 3). Roland continues to serve as chairman of the advisory board of the Association of Regional Currencies in Germany. And our mutual interests in networked organizations, complementary currencies, and TOYF keep us firmly connected.

### Adina Luca

When we asked our first client in Romania what company they might recommend to represent us, they recommended Adina's company. That was the beginning of our relationship. There have been many twists and turns in Adina's career—so much so that I label her e-mail file "Adina's Adventures."

Today, Adina is one of the founders of Stillae, where she is a strategic consultant. That means helping clients make the most from their financial data by aligning structures and processes with strategy and then using data to create feedback systems. Prior to Stillae, Adina was an associate partner with Gallup, where she helped organizations across Europe implement employee and customer engagement programs.

She has published a book on management culture in Romania and consulted on cross-cultural management for large European multinationals.

She indulges her passion for research by studying the dynamics of networks. The results of this research are reported in resource 3.

Adina has a master's degree in psychotherapy and counseling from City University, United Kingdom, and a bachelor's degree in language and literature from the University of Bucharest, Romania. She is currently studying for a postgraduate diploma in human resource management at Seneca College of Applied Arts and Technology, Canada.

## Peter Everett

I met Peter Everett at a very early age: he is my son. We didn't spend much time together during his teenage years, so we are making up for it now.

In 1989, with an economics degree under his belt, Peter set off backpacking around the world. In 3 years on the move, he learned fundamental lessons about life, death, and love.

His first introduction to real work was with Bankers Trust Australia, a successful merchant bank. After a few years Peter was a voluntary corporate refugee. In a quest for more meaning in his career, he started working with school children in outdoor-based camps. This led to corporate outdoor experiential training.

In 1996, he traveled to Singapore to try out working with me. During this period, he became severely ill with malaria during a conference on the Great Wall of China. (The malaria was caught elsewhere.) Nursing him, literally, during this period and being evacuated by chartered jet to Hong Kong brought us together in new ways. Finally, Pete decided he *could* work with me.

Today, Peter is CEO of our company, which means he is the hub and general go-to guy for TOYFNET throughout Asia-Pacific and India. In his day-to-day work he lives and breathes all aspects of this book. Peter delights in the friendships, the challenges, and the surprises the network brings.

To Ric, Jacqueline, Roland, Adina, and Peter I simply say, "Thank you!"

## How Can We Continue Our Conversation?

We'd be pleased to continue this conversation. There are three ways to do so:

- Visit http://www.n2nhub.com for more resources.
- Contact me at ken@n2nhub.com.
- Contact Peter at peter@n2nhub.com.

# Notes

## Preface

1. Perkin (2010).

## Chapter 1

1. Hamel (2010a).
2. Visa (2011).
3. Glassdoor.com (2009). Glassdoor is a website that allows, among other things, employees to submit feedback about their employers.
4. Glassdoor.com (2010).
5. Hock (2005), p. ix.
6. A question you might have is "How do you pronounce 'TOYFNET'?" Simply imagine it as two syllables, "toyf" and "net," run together, and the "toyf" part can be said just like one would say "toys," but with an "f" instead of an "s."
7. Think on Your Feet® is a registered trademark of Think on Your Feet International, Inc.
8. See http://www.thinkonyourfeet.com and resource 6.
9. Vickers (1983) as quoted in Hames (1994), p. 73.
10. Semler (1995).
11. Cross and Parker (2004), p. 5.
12. Cross and Parker (2001). Reprinted with permission from Elsevier Science.

## Chapter 3

1. Gribbin (2005), pp. 2–3.
2. As noted at http://en.wikipedia.org/wiki/Bernard-Lietaer#cite_note-3. See also www.lietaer.com/2010/02curriculum-vitae.
3. Lietaer (2001); emphasis mine.
4. Lietaer, Ulanowicz, and Goerner (2008), p. 1.
5. Pink (2010).
6. Slideshare (2004).
7. Slideshare (2004).

# Chapter 4

1. Vickers (1983).
2. Granovetter (1973).
3. Pink (2009).

# Chapter 5

1. We'd not yet dreamed up the name TOYFNET. I substitute it here for clarity.
2. Owen (2008).
3. Brown and Isaacs (2005).
4. Godin (2008).
5. Axelrod (1990), ch. 9.

# Chapter 6

1. *The Sydney Magazine* (February 2011), p. 68.
2. Rauch (1995).
3. Waldrop (1996), p. 75.
4. Waldrop (1996), p. 75.
5. Waldrop (1996), p. 75.
6. Wieners (2004), p. 2.
7. Block (2008a), p. 85.
8. Kohn (1999), p. 181.
9. Pink (2009), p. 88.
10. Sutton (2011).
11. Sutton (2010), p. 3.
12. Block (2008b).
13. Limerick and Cunnington (1993), p. 37.
14. Limerick and Cunnington (1993), p. 37.
15. Power (2010).
16. Dawkins (1973), pp. 203–215.
17. Davis (1987), p. 5.
18. Stewart (2009), p. 57.
19. Wheatley (1992).
20. Reynolds (1986).

# Chapter 7

1. Semler (2004).
2. Granovetter (2003).
3. Cross and Parker (2004).
4. Pink (2009), pp. 86–88.

# Chapter 8

1. Pink (2009).
2. Limerick and Cunnington (1993).
3. Gallup (2011).
4. Cross and Parker (2004).

# Chapter 9

1. SAP Community Network (2010).
2. Levine et al. (2000), p. 75.
3. Turnbull (2002), p. 5.
4. Semler (1995).
5. Semler (2005).
6. Semler (2004).
7. Hock (2005), p. ix.
8. Bughin, Chui, and Manyika (2010).

# Chapter 10

1. Hamel (2010b).
2. Hamel (2010a).
3. Lee (2011), pp. 27–28.
4. Turnbull (2002), p. 2.
5. Hock (2005), p. 242.
6. Curtis (1990), p. 7.
7. Deci (1999), as quoted in Pink (2009), p. 70 and p. 39.
8. Handy (1995), p. 230.
9. Roberts et al. (2006).
10. Blue (2010).

# Resource 1

1. Douthwaite (1999).
2. Curtis (1990), p 10.
3. Pink (2009), pp. 72–73.
4. Pink (2009), p. 203.
5. Blanchflower and Oswald (2004).
6. Semler (1995).

# Resource 3

1. Luca (2005).
2. For information on grounded theory, see Glaser and Strauss (1967).

# Resource 5

1. Semler (1995).

# Resource 6

1. For more, see http://www.thinkonyourfeet.com.
2. As of 2011, the European business returns to McLuhan & Davies.

# References

Axelrod, R. (1990). *The evolution of cooperation*. London, UK: Penguin.

Blanchflower, D. G., & Oswald, A. (2004). Money, sex and happiness: An empirical study. *Scandinavian Journal of Economics 106*(3), 393–415.

Block, P. (2008a). *Community: The structure of belonging*. San Francisco, CA: Berrett-Koehler.

Block, P. (2008b). *Community: The structure of belonging*. Session conducted at the ASTD International Conference and Exhibition, San Diego, CA.

Blue, L. (2010, July 28). Recipe for longevity: No smoking, lots of friends. *Time Magazine*. Retrieved February 18, 2011, from http://www.time.com/time/health/article/0,8599,2006938,00.html

Brown, J., & Isaacs, D. (2005). *The world café*. San Francisco, CA: Berrett-Koehler.

Bughin, J., Chui, M., & Manyika, J. (2010, August). Clouds, big data, and smart assets: Ten tech-enabled business trends to watch. *McKinsey Quarterly*. Retrieved April 30, 2011, from https://www.mckinseyquarterly.com/High_Tech/Strategy_Analysis/Clouds_big_data_and_smart_assets_Ten_tech-enabled_business_trends_to_watch_2647

Carney, B. M., & Getz, I. (2009). *Freedom Inc*. New York, NY: Crown Business.

Cross, R., & Parker, A. (2004). *The hidden power of social networks*. Boston, MA: Harvard Business School Press.

Cross, R., & Parker, A. (2001). Knowing what we know: Supporting knowledge creation and sharing in social networks. *Organizational Dynamics 30*(2), 100–120.

Curtis, D. A. (1990). *Management rediscovered: How companies can escape the numbers trap*. Homewood, IL: Dow-Jones Irwin.

Davis, S. M. (1987). *Future perfect*. New York, NY: Addison-Wesley.

Dawkins, R. (1973). *The selfish gene*. New York, NY: Oxford University Press.

Douthwaite, R. (1999). *The ecology of money*. Devon, UK: Green Books for the Schumacher Society.

Gallup (2011). *Employee engagement*. Retrieved April 30, 2011, from http://www.gallup.com/consulting/52/employee-engagement.aspx

Glaser, B. G., & Strauss, A. L. (1967). *The discovery of grounded theory: Strategies for qualitative research*. Chicago, IL: Aldine Publishing.

Glassdoor. (2009). *IPO changed everything*. Retrieved April 30, 2011, from http://www.glassdoor.com/Reviews/Visa-Inc-Company-Reviews-E3035_P9.htm

Glassdoor. (2010). *Still happy to be at Visa*. Retrieved April 30, 2011, from http://www.glassdoor.com/Reviews/Visa-Inc-Company-Reviews-E3035_P5 .htm

Godin, S. (2008). *Tribes*. New York, NY: Portfolio.

Granovetter, M. (1973). The strength of weak ties. *American Journal of Sociology*, *78*(6), 1360–1380.

Gribbin, J. (2005). *Deep simplicity*. London, UK: Penguin.

Hamel, G. (2010a). *Why can't we build organizations that are highly adaptable, endlessly inventive, and truly inspiring?* [Video file]. Retrieved July 31, 2010, from http://www.managementinnovationexchange.com

Hamel, G. (2010b, November 5). Imperious institutions, impotent individuals. *Management Innovation Exchange*. Retrieved February 18, 2011, from http:// www.managementexchange.com/blog/trust/imperious-institutions-impotent -individuals

Hames, R. D. (1994). *The management myth*. Sydney, Australia: Business and Professional Publishing.

Handy, C. (1995). *The empty raincoat*. London, UK: Arrow Business Books.

Hock, D. (2005). *One from many*. San Francisco, CA: Berret-Koehler.

Kohn, A. (1999). *Punished by rewards*. Boston, MA: Houghton Mifflin.

Lee, A. (2011). The world in 2011. *The Economist's* predictions summarized. Retrieved February 18, 2011, from http://www.chilliwebsites.com/sitefiles/ 3064/File/The%20World%20in%202011.pdf

Levine, R., Locke, C., Searles, D., & Weinberg, D. (2000). *The cluetrain manifesto*. Cambridge, MA: Perseus Books.

Lietaer, B. (2001). *The future of money*. London, UK: Random House.

Lietaer, B., Ulanowicz, R., & Goerner, S. (2008, October 22). *Options for managing systemic bank crises*. Paper for the World Academy of Arts and Sciences, Hyderabad, India.

Limerick, D. C., & Cunnington, B. (1993). *Managing the new organization*. Chatswood, Australia: Business & Professional Publishing.

Luca, A. (2005). *Employeescu*. Bucharest, Romania: Pur si Simplu.

Owen, H. (2008). *Open space technology*. San Francisco, CA: Berrett-Koehler.

Perkin, C. (2010). *A bite in the tale: Interview with Brian Guthrie*. Retrieved April 30, 2010, from http://www.theweeklyreview.com.au/article-display/ A-bite-in-the-tale/3332

Pink, D. (2009). *Drive*. New York, NY: Riverhead.

Pink, D. (2010). *RSA Animate - Drive: The surprising truth about what motivates us*. [Video file]. Retrieved April 30, 2011, from http://www.youtube.com/ watch?v=u6XAPnuFjJc

Power, T. (2010). *Open, random, supportive*. [Video file]. Retrieved February 4, 2011, from http://www.youtube.com/watch?v=S4IpLo0rKkE

Rauch, J. (1995, December 23) Short guys finish last. *The Economist*. Retrieved April 30, 2011, from http://www.jonathanrauch.com/jrauch_articles/2004/08/short_guys_fini.html

Reynolds, C. (1986). *Boids*. Retrieved February 4, 2011, from http://www.red3d.com/cwr/boids

Roberts, L., Dutton, J., Speitzer, G., & Suisse, J. (2006). *Bringing my reflected best self to life*. Ann Arbor, MI: Stephen M. Ross School of Business, University of Michigan. Retrieved February 18, 2011, from http://www.bus.umich.edu/positive/PDF/RBS-Exercise-booklet-RL-review-copy.pdf

SAP Community Network. (2010). Guided tour. Retrieved February 5, 2011, from http://www.sdn.sap.com/irj/scn/elearn?rid=/library/uuid/703385a5-7039-2d10-12b5-dcbc2df6d25b

Semler, R. (1995). *Maverick*. New York, NY: Warner Books.

Semler, R. (2004). *The seven-day weekend*. New York, NY: Portfolio.

Semler, R. (2005). *Leading by omission* [Video file]. Retrieved February 11, 2011, http://mitworld.mit.edu/video/308

Slideshare (2004). *Netflix culture*. Retrieved April 29, 2011, from http://www.slideshare.net/ASCHUT/culture9090801103430phpapp02-1911634

Stewart, M. (2009). *The management myth*. New York, NY: W. W. Norton.

Sutton, R. I. (2010, August). Why good bosses tune in to their people. *McKinsey Quarterly*. Retrieved February 4, 2011, from https://www.mckinseyquarterly.com/Why_good_bosses_tune_in_to_their_people_2656

Sutton, R. I. (2011). Who's the boss in an open world? *Management Innovation Exchange*. Retrieved February 4, 2011, from http://www.managementexchange.com/video/whos-boss-open-world

Think on Your Feet International. (n.d.). Retrieved December 10, 2010, from http://www.thinkonyourfeet.com

Turnbull, S. (2002). *A new way to govern*. London: NEF Pocketbook 6. Retrieved December 10, 2010, from http://www.neweconomics.org/publications

Vickers, G. (1983). *Human systems are different*. London, UK: Harper & Row.

Visa. (2011). History of Visa. Retrieved December 11, 2010, from http://corporate.visa.com/about-visa/our-business/history-of-visa.shtml

Waldrop, M. M. (1996, November). The trillion dollar vision of Dee Hock. *Fast Company* 5, 75. Retrieved April 30, 2011, from http://www.fastcompany.com/magazine/05/deehock.html?page=0%2C0

Wheatley, M. J. (1992). *Leadership and the new science*. San Francisco, CA: Berrett-Koehler.

Wieners, B. (2004, April). Ricardo Semler: Set them free. Retrieved April 30, 2011, from http://www.cioinsight.com/c/a/Expert-Voices/Ricardo-Semler-Set-Them-Free

# Index

Note: The italicized *f* and *t* following page numbers refers to figures and tables respectively.

# Announcing the Business Expert Press Digital Library

*Concise E-books Business Students Need for Classroom and Research*

This book can also be purchased in an e-book collection by your library as

- a one-time purchase,
- that is owned forever,
- allows for simultaneous readers,
- has no restrictions on printing, and
- can be downloaded as PDFs from within the library community.

Our digital library collections are a great solution to beat the rising cost of textbooks. E-books can be loaded into their course management systems or onto students' e-book readers.

The **Business Expert Press** digital libraries are very affordable, with no obligation to buy in future years.

For more information, please visit **www.businessexpertpress.com/librarians**. To set up a trial in the United States, please contact **Sheri Allen** at *sheri.allen@globalepress.com*; for all other regions, contact **Nicole Lee** at *nicole.lee@igroupnet.com*.

---

## OTHER TITLES IN OUR STRATEGIC MANAGEMENT COLLECTION
### Collection Editor: **Mason A. Carpenter**

Building Strategy and Performance Through Time: The Critical Path by Kim Warren

Sustainable Business: An Executive's Primer by Nancy Landrum and Sally Edwards

Mergers and Acquisitions: Turmoil in Top Management Teams by Jeffrey Krug

Positive Management: Increasing Employee Productivity by Jack Walters

Business Goes Virtual: Realizing the Value of Collaboration, Social and Virtual Strategies by John Girard and JoAnn Girard

Fundamentals of Global Strategy: A Business Model Approach by Cornelis de Kluyver

Grow by Focusing on What Matters: Competitive Strategy in 3-Circles by Joe Urbany and Jim Davis

Operational Leadership by Andrew Spanyi

Succeeding at the Top: A Self-Paced Workbook for Newly Appointed CEOs and Executives by Bernard Liebowitz

Achieving Excellence in Management: Identifying and Learning from Bad Practices by Andrew Kilner

Building Organizational Capacity for Change: The Leader's New Mandate by William Q. Judge

Crafting Strategy by M. Akbar and Mahesh P. Joshi

Executing Strategy: People, Processes and Projects by Mahesh P. Joshi and M. Akbar

Business Intelligence: Making Decisions Through Data Analytics by Jerzy Surma

CPSIA information can be obtained at www.ICGtesting.com
Printed in the USA
BVOW051350190911

271438BV00005B/2/P